Conversations on Humanity and Creativity

ALSO AVAILABLE FROM BLOOMSBURY:

Humanism, by Anthony B. Pinn
Secularity and Nonreligion in North America, Edited by Jesse M. Smith and Ryan T. Cragun
American Druidry, by Kimberly Kirner

Humanism, at its best, is a creative and secular exploration of what it means to be human. No one understands this better – or has achieved more in the field of humanist studies – than Anthony B. Pinn, a legend among those who care about the positive values, histories, cultures, and communities of nonreligious people. These dialogues showcase Pinn at his most conversational and relevant.

> GREG M. EPSTEIN, *Humanist Chaplain at Harvard University and the Massachusetts Institute of Technology, USA*

Conversations on Humanity and Creativity is that rare thing - a scholarly book that is not only full of innovative thought, but it also explores waves of imaginative and playful expression. Anthony B. Pinn has cleverly curated a text that demonstrates the power of conversation; a mode of engagement that demonstrates conviviality and civility, outlining the best of the mythical Salon as a space for appreciative enquiry. In an age of destructive and combative polarisation, *Conversations on Humanity and Creativity* reveals an alternative and joyful means of engagement. This is a must read!

> ANTHONY G. REDDIE, *University of Oxford, UK*

These fascinating conversations range widely across different areas, held together by a focus on human creativity and by Dr. Anthony B. Pinn's dedication to the art of dialogue. From his interlocutors Dr. Pinn draws out personal histories, accounts of artistic production, and trenchant reflections on religion and Black secularism.

> ANDREW C. DOLE, *Amherst College, USA*

Beautiful! This book is written in a way to pique the reader's curiosity while satisfying their craving for connection without employing a particular set of mastered dialogue skills. It is an invitation for people to engage in conversation about the mundane, fascinating, and wonder of life and humanity that allows us to simply be and understand one another. What a gift!

> SABRINA E. DENT, *Director of the BJC Center for Faith, Justice and Reconciliation, USA*

Conversations on Humanity and Creativity

Edited by
ANTHONY B. PINN

BLOOMSBURY ACADEMIC
LONDON • NEW YORK • OXFORD • NEW DELHI • SYDNEY

BLOOMSBURY ACADEMIC

Bloomsbury Publishing Plc, 50 Bedford Square, London, WC1B 3DP, UK
Bloomsbury Publishing Inc, 1359 Broadway, 12th Floor, New York, NY 10018, USA
Bloomsbury Publishing Ireland, 29 Earlsfort Terrace, Dublin 2, D02 AY28, Ireland

BLOOMSBURY, BLOOMSBURY ACADEMIC and the Diana logo are trademarks of
Bloomsbury Publishing Plc

First published in Great Britain 2026

Copyright © Anthony B. Pinn and contributors, 2026

Anthony B. Pinn has asserted his right under the Copyright, Designs and Patents Act, 1988,
to be identified as Author of this work.

For legal purposes the Acknowledgments on p. xiv constitute an extension
of this copyright page.

Cover design: Jade Barnett

This work is published open access subject to a Creative Commons Attribution-
NonCommercial-NoDerivatives 4.0 International licence (CC BY-NC-ND 4.0, https://
creativecommons.org/licenses/by-nc-nd/4.0/). You may re-use, distribute, and reproduce
this work in any medium for non-commercial purposes, provided you give attribution to the
copyright holder and the publisher and provide a link to the Creative Commons licence.

Bloomsbury Publishing Plc does not have any control over, or responsibility for, any third-
party websites referred to or in this book. All internet addresses given in this book were
correct at the time of going to press. The author and publisher regret any inconvenience
caused if addresses have changed or sites have ceased to exist, but can accept no
responsibility for any such changes.

A catalogue record for this book is available from the British Library.

A catalog record for this book is available from the Library of Congress.

ISBN: HB: 978-1-3505-2717-1
PB: 978-1-3505-2716-4
ePDF: 978-1-3505-2718-8
eBook: 978-1-3505-2719-5

Typeset by Deanta Global Publishing Services, Chennai, India
Printed and bound in Great Britain

For product safety related questions contact productsafety@bloomsbury.com.

To find out more about our authors and books visit www.bloomsbury.com
and sign up for our newsletters.

Dedicated
to
Those Who Make Worlds with Words

Contents

List of Figures xi
Contributors xii
Acknowledgments xiv
Note on Presentation xv

Introduction 1

PART I Creatively Human 13

1 Grieving While Disbelieving *Candace Gorham* 15

2 When to Walk, When to Fight *Nadya Dutchin* 31

3 Freethought and Black Personhood *Christopher Cameron* 41

4 Seeing the Secular *Phil Zuckerman* 53

PART II Human Creativity 69

5 "The Afrofuturistic Gardener" *Angelbert Metoyer* 71

6 A Serious Sense of Play *Jamal Cyrus* 81

7 Art Imitating Life *Jeremiah Camara* 95

8 The Raw Truth of Hip Hop *Harry Allen* 105

9 We're Still Here! *Valerie Cassel Oliver* 119

10 On Black AI *Philip Butler* 133

Notes 143
Index 153

Figures

5.1 Icon Execution, Coal dust, oil, and paper on canvas, 2010. 75
5.2 Black Devil in Berlin, Coal dust and graphite on artist washed paper, 2014. 78
6.1 Misconstrued Rap Lyric #1, Triple beam balance, painted plaster bust of D. Martin Luther King, shelf 20 × 19 × 6 inches, 2019. 84
6.2 Pride Frieze-Jerry White's Record Shop, Central Avenue, Los Angeles, 2005–17 collage on album cover, acrylic paint, plywood, wax, plexiglas 121.24 × 126.5 × 12 inches. 87
6.3 Lights from the Garden, Bentwood chairs, stainless steel rods, oak flooring 74 × 87.5 × 31.75 inches, 2019. 89
6.4 Medicated Shield, wooden pew, mandingas, sand bags 35.25 × 84 × 23.5 inches, 2021. 90
6.5 Inner Necessity to Outer Time (Run Mary Run), denim, cotton thread, burlap 84 × 84 inchemode_comments, 2021. 91

Contributors

Harry Allen is an internationally known Hip Hop activist and journalist. He is an advisor to the Archives of African American Music and Culture at Indiana University.

Philip Butler is Associate Professor of Theology and Black Posthuman Artificial Intelligence Systems at Iliff School of Theology, Denver, CO. He is the author of *Black Transhuman Liberation Theology: Spirituality and Technology*.

Jeremiah Camara is an author and filmmaker living in Atlanta, Georgia. His most recent film is *Holy Hierarchy: The Religious Roots of Racism in America*.

Christopher Cameron is Professor of History and African American Studies at the University of North Carolina-Charlotte. He is the author of *Black Freethinkers: A History of African American Secularism*.

Jamal Cyrus is an award-winning artist and former member of the collective Otabenga Jones and Associates. He is also a professor at Texas Southern University.

Nadya Dutchin is Executive Director of ShareBaby, an organization that works to meet the needs of young children in Baltimore by distributing essential items.

Candace Gorham is a mental health professional and secular activist. She is the author of *On Death, Dying and Disbelief*.

Angelbert Metoyer uses a multimedia approach to issues of memory, history, and family. His work is held in the permanent collection of institutions such as the US State Department and the Houston Museum of Fine Art.

Valerie Cassel Oliver is the Sydney and Frances Lewis Family Curator of Modern and Contemporary Art at the Virginia Museum of Fine Arts. An award-winning curator, she is also the editor of the highly regarded *The Dirty South: Contemporary Art, Material Culture, and the Sonic Impulse*.

Anthony B. Pinn is the Agnes Cullen Arnold Distinguished Professor of Humanities and Professor of Religion at Rice University, where he also directs the Center for Engaged Research and Collaborative Learning.

Phil Zuckerman is Professor of Sociology and Secular Studies and Associate Dean of Faculty at Pitzer College. He is the author of *What It Means to Be Moral*.

Acknowledgments

This book was a long time in the making, and I want to take this opportunity to thank all those who helped me move from a series of audio conversations to this published book. First, a big thank you to Dale McGowan and the folks at OnlySky Media for inviting me to develop and host the podcast that ultimately became this book. That was a fantastic experience, thanks Dale! I've worked with Lalle Pursglove for a good number of years now, and each experience has been fantastic. Thank you Lalle, Seb Claas, and the rest of the Bloomsbury team for another fantastically smooth and enjoyable publishing process. I'm also grateful to the reviewers whose comments and suggestions made this book better. This work is published open access with funding from William Marsh Rice University, USA.

I must also thank the wonderful people who agreed to be guests on that podcast and who allowed me to include those conversations in this book. They are all wonderful, creative, inspiring thinkers, and I'm sure you'll learn as much from them as I did. Thank you to Candace Gorham, Nadya Dutchin, Christopher Cameron, Phil Zuckerman, Angelbert Metoyer, Jamal Cyrus, Jeremiah Camara, Harry Allen, Valerie Cassel Oliver, and Philip Butler. Y'all are the best!

Moving from transcripts of these conversations to book chapters took a great deal of work, and it involved some heavy lifting on the part of Maya Reine. Thanks, Maya!

Finally, I owe a debt of gratitude and appreciation to family and friends for their love and support! Much appreciated. Much Love.

Anthony B. Pinn

Note on Presentation

These chapters, first offered as audio interviews related to my podcast, remain conversations in the form of an interview. Nothing has been changed in terms of content other than what was needed to make them function within a print format—for example, consistent capitalization of Black and removing redundancies. Other than that fine-tuning, I added reference information where I thought it would be useful to readers.

Introduction

> Conversation doesn't have to lead to consensus about anything, especially not values; it's enough that it helps people get used to one another.
>
> —Kwame Anthony Appiah

Better than a decade ago psychologist and MIT professor Sherry Turkle lamented in the *New York Times* the decline of conversation occasioned by other, more technological, forms of "connection." Exploring the phenomenon of disengaged closeness precipitated by advances such as the text message and email, Turkle notes:

> Human relationships are rich; they're messy and demanding. We have learned the habit of cleaning them up with technology. And the move from conversation to connection is part of this. But it's a process in which we shortchange ourselves. Worse, it seems that over time we stop caring, we forget that there is a difference. . . . In conversation, we are called upon to see things from another's point of view.[1]

Turkle is not alone in this assessment that recent advances in technologically facilitated engagement fall flat because they tend to smooth out the complexities of human engagement. Others also point to something about understanding ourselves and understanding others involving discernment requiring conversation as a practice informed by the intricacies of our existence. This entails dialogue that doesn't assume commonality or sameness as the prerequisite for exchange, but rather digs at and into issues from our various vantage points. For instance, this, it seems, is what Anthony Appiah is getting at in the quotation at the start of this introduction.

When People Talk

In all honesty, what Turkle frames in terms of the downside of technology use captures some of my approach with friends and family—with whom I am faster with a text message than a phone call. Memories of those folks play out in my mind, as it tries to keep pace with my fingers tapping out responses as I also review email, edit a paper, take a long walk, or watch TV. Multitasking as my fingers glide across the iPhone screen in an effort to maintain emotional connections with those at a distance (on their own devices). Yet, despite my use of technology as a type of buffer that shapes and manages time and contact, in a more general sense I've become increasingly sensitive to the centrality of direct and "raw" conversation for fostering clarity as well as greater awareness of the world in which we live, the ways in which we have structured our relationship to that world, and what remains for us to do. This is not to say I'm going to call more and text less; no, rather, this sensitivity is reflected first in my professional work involving an effort to move between my more traditionally academic writing projects and those prioritizing less filtered engagement with others.[2] Regarding the latter, the goal of conversation is a process of exchange in which possibilities remain wildly open.

Paula Marantz Cohen speaks to this when reflecting on the loss of diverse conversation that years ago was tied to the very act of living resulting from "the serendipity of having to move around in literal space created unpredictable encounters. People were forced to engage with others in order to carry on the business of their lives"; but,

> that element of serendipity has now diminished. For all our espousal of difference and diversity, we have become a nation of faction and tribes, our thinking, in so many instances, hardened into repetitive patterns of agreement or opposition. The rise of social media, while it provides access to people in far-flung places, also supports a narrow sectarianism of ideas and feeds mockery and mean-spiritedness. . . . Many people nowadays engage only with those whose views and life experiences mirror their own.[3]

When controlling for the nostalgia marking those remarks, there are benefits to diverse engagement—some of which are intellectual to be sure. We are opened more widely to what we value, what we foster, and what we create (and the "why" of creation). What I am suggesting is that conversation provides a window into our creative selves—that is, the ways in which we imagine worlds and then allow materialized imaginings to occupy those worlds. I'm not suggesting conversation creates creativity, so to speak; rather, conversation is an intriguing way to gain greater perspective on the nature of creativity by offering opportunity to recognize and interrogate the context, content, and meaning (the "why") of what we produce.[4]

Based on the assumption that dialogue affords a much richer understanding of human activity than one can gather from detached reflection, this volume explores how humans engage the world—both shaping and being shaped by it. Undergirding, or anchoring, these conversations is a guiding question: What might we learn by talking with a range of creatives—some atheistic, some theistic, some for whom such labels are of limited value—about issues that animate their work and life? For some of those in the volume, creativity is tied to vertical considerations and for others creativity is tied to a horizontal plane. For those in the volume who believe in some type of higher power or adhere to a framework of spirituality, human creativity manifests in relationship to a force beyond humans as a vertical relationship to possibility. For those without theological beliefs, human creativity is restricted to human knowledge, capacity, and resources as a horizontal relationship to possibility. Why is it important to offer this brief framing of my conversation partners in terms of their relationship to theological claims? Because the aim of this volume isn't to simply affirm a particular ideological position but rather, as philosopher Albert Camus encourages, to think and represent the value of conversation engaged by people as they are. Such an approach here also offers opportunity to see human creativity from within and in light of various philosophical vantage points and with regard to their corresponding epistemological frameworks.

Processes of imaginative "making" involve more than mechanisms by which need is addressed—for example, tools forged, structures built, physical barriers arranged. Instead, I want to understand creativity as not simply the production of devices used by humans but rather the expression of imagination with more existential and ontological purchase. Hence, materialization of imagination as I mean it addresses more foundational concerns in that it involves not what humans use but how humans think and represent themselves in relationship to a living world. Presenting creativity so understood and in an expansive manner—for example, music, the visual arts, writing and coding, ritual practices, academic exploration, and film—the conversations in this book name and tap into what it means to be human by focusing on what humans do, and why they do what they do. In a word, these conversations present human creativity in light of a range of life contexts, professional affiliations, and social-cultural worlds. And I go along for the ride.

I make that last statement not to blur the nature of my involvement as the one who selected participants and who provided the questions guiding the conversations. No, instead, it is meant to suggest the sense of mutuality at work by which we enable ourselves to entertain "the multiple voices of creative and expressive humanity."[5] I've made an effort to shape the themes (so as to allow some focus), but not define the full content. And while I know and have worked with those in this volume, our connection isn't simply a matter of sociocultural sameness. There are things about which we disagree because of dissimilar ideological leanings or life experiences. Still, the goal isn't persuasion but understanding—connection that allows for greater complexity of thought, which is a type of communicative openness. I believe my connection to those in this book entails deep appreciation for processes and patterns of human creativity, and a desire to better understand what this all says to, for, and about us. In other words:

> conversation is both a function of and a metaphor for our life in the world, always seeking to fulfill a need that is never fulfilled but whose quest gives piquancy and satisfaction, albeit temporarily and incompletely, to our encounters. In a good conversation, there is always something left out, unplumbed, and unresolved, which is why we seek more of it.[6]

More on Creativity

I make no claim that conversation alone transforms our circumstances, alters our condition, or transcends limitations. Rather, I argue conversation offers, to borrow again from Camus, moments of greater awareness, of greater clarity, regarding existential and ontological arrangements that seem to define human life. And that epistemological increase, in and of itself, makes conversation worthwhile—animating us one exchange at a time, highlighting the "poetic" quality of our encounters with each other with/in the world, and in the process pointing out something "new."[7]

Hip Hop artists, for instance, take music, images, clothing, dance moves, and so on, and transform them. And, in that way, foster new possibilities of encounter that expose dynamics of life often ignored—that is, signifying as creative expression. Coming out of the world of Hip Hop, the artist Basquiat, for instance, exemplified creativity as a restructuring of what constitutes the linguistic and visual practices of the social world by turning them on their head—thereby freeing them to tell other, more critical stories. Basquiat and other creatives take the ordinary and push us to see a depth of expression and possibility—to see the world anew from within the context of the ordinary. The power, at least in part, of creativity is for me it's unruliness—our inability to fully capture it, to restrict it linguistically or to capture it fully through a confined set of practices.[8] It is an open process with the capacity for good or harm because creativity pushes to the depth of human possibility without a particular moral or ethical mandate. That directive comes later with interpretation or application. For this book, this second step surfaces on occasion as we talk about the values displayed in particular situations. Some of the implications of this question of values are left underdeveloped in these conversations, and this is because the purpose here isn't to obtain a particular strategy for engaging the political, but rather for simply gaining greater understanding of what humans "make" and why these things are "made" in a more metaphysical sense. Creativity pulls from something much deeper than that—than the political utility of things. Utility involves inspiration; yet, there is an important distinction between inspiration and creativity. The latter, creativity, as I mean it, involves a more elemental wrestling, a re/structuring more along the lines of how humans process and respond to the fundamental issues of our existence. In this way, the "product" points outward as well as inward—saying something about the humanness of the "creative" and the world(s) encountered. It is more than how to make physical space comfortable and sustainable, and instead is concerned with how we interact in that space and what we say about the nature and meaning of our humanity in the process of occupying time and space.

While there are various disciplinary perspectives on creativity, I tend toward the Humanities.[9] What Zadie Smith says concerning writing is, I believe, applicable to a broader framing of creativity as I mean it: "To my mind, a true 'creative' should not simply seek to satisfy a pre-existing demand but instead transform our notion of what it is we want."[10] Or, one might move away from the dynamic of creativity dealing with the exploding of assumptions concerning the fixity of our identities, to what we *do* based on the complexities of being and thinking about creativity as having dynamics captured by what Zora Neale Hurston called "hitting a straight lick with a crooked stick."[11] This is the process of transforming what is in order to draw out what might be. Such transformative effort takes many forms. And so, then, creativity is a broad category capturing the intentional structuring—the vibrant aftermath—of human imagination in a range of ways. One might tie this deep work to what historian Robin Kelley, in *Freedom Dreams*, describes as the human imaginative process of freedom work. What Kelley speaks to is the significance and inherent value of vision, of imagined new worlds despite the persistence of troubling circumstances.[12]

Although not identical to my take on creativity, there is something to Kelley's celebration of vision that resembles my interest in the disruptive power of creativity to amplify our self-awareness in connection to others. His sense of vision and my framing of creativity suggest a particular posture toward the world—a certain type of engagement with experience expressed in various forms. I find something useful for naming and understanding creativity in his seeing "life as possibility . . . the poetic and prophetic in the richness of our daily lives."[13] In both cases—vision and creativity—engagement and the process of "making" involve an interrogation and detangling of ourselves from what has been assumed necessary. One way of putting this—I realize the limitations of the language—is creativity as I mean it, and vision as Kelley names it, serve to enhance our humanity through greater regard for and structuring of how we touch the world and how we are touched by all that's in the world. Such thinking raises a host of questions that inform creative practices: Who are we? What are we doing in and for the world? Who do we want to be? What matters most? Or, least?[14]

My interviewees and I bring ourselves to these conversations—our identities shaped as they are by our experiences within the context, for example, of both voluntary (i.e., social networks and communities) and involuntary associations (e.g., our status within the US capitalist system) that give form to the whole of our being. We speak and respond in light of this network of connections and what those connections say to and about human creativity. My interviewees, like myself, would tend to identify as progressives. Yet, our conversations are more focused on what humans make and what that making says about us, rather than the proper political and economic platform for human society vis-à-vis creativity. We are exploring creativity in light of how it emerges without significant preoccupation with formal political constraints (or guardrails) that might inform creative expression. Of course, the sociopolitical and economic are always present in some sense, and this is unavoidable. However, the aim here isn't to develop a unified approach to such concerns, or to view conversation as simply a tool for sociopolitical ends. *In these pages the conversations are the point, not a means to the point.* This limitation might frustrate some readers who pick up this book assuming answers to the current litany of challenges. Still, I hope those readers will find in these pages an affirmation of life's integrity that, while not fulfilling their desire for a systematic activist agenda, helps to express the imaginative processes (i.e., creativity) that undergird our movement through the world.[15] We are able to have these exchanges *not* despite networks that name and situate us, but in relationship to these similarities and differences. We are both connected and disconnected at the same time.

As I read them, authors like Timothy Stacey explore voluntary and involuntary associations and what they say concerning our willingness to cooperate for the purpose of finding what might prove transformative beyond our individual realities.[16] Stacey, for example, laments what he perceives as an unwillingness on the part of many to fully comprehend the impact of involuntary associations to the degree we assume the only meaningful associations are constituted by volunteered connections. And, by extension of that logic, in leaving or embracing involuntary associations, we, as individuals, are able to shape our circumstances. While I differ with Stacey on a variety of fronts (e.g., the nature and meaning of religion and religious experience, or the general utility of theological derived frameworks), I appreciate the call for more robust exchanges on the impactful circumstances of life and, I would agree, this might have something to do with religion.[17] Some might raise questions concerning how fairly religion as a source of creativity is dealt with in this book, particularly in light of my decidedly secular humanistic orientation and that of many of the interviewees.[18] Again, as readers will discover, the role or importance of religion (defined in a variety of ways) differs across the following conversations. For some, religion (i.e., vertical concerns) is a key factor in defining their artistic and intellectual practices. For others, religion isn't a consideration (i.e., horizontal concerns). Regarding the place of religion in human creativity, I follow the lead of my interviewees and make an effort not to impose my thinking.

Furthermore, while Stacey seems concerned with the outcomes promoted by political participation and communal exchange, I am interested in a more limited consideration: What are some of the ways in which human creativity (i.e., as the materialization of imagination in the form of concretely projected markers of human meaning) is expressed and how is its expression articulated and understood across differing philosophies of life and existential orientations? To the extent values come up in these conversations, we tend to be reflecting on principles represented within particular examples of creativity and not—like Stacey—making explicit judgments concerning the "correctness" or utility of those values. For me such activities are vital, but they tame what I mean by creativity by lodging it only—or almost exclusively—in the functional, or in what is easily processed and manipulated.

Again, for the purposes of this book, creativity is more than problem-solving in that it involves an act beyond the mechanics of existential convenience. It isn't simply utilitarian—although it can involve some dimension or level of this. Creativity contains an element of desire that isn't restricted to function in that it, in some sense, encourages an expansion of who we are—opening us to a deeper regard for the nature and meaning of life (within our context of death). I think some of what I mean here is captured in Camus' understanding of art—extended to creativity more generally—as exposing the human effort to be other than what we are. Which is to say the effort to be more than our circumstances, to be aware of possibility.[19] Creativity involves an interrogation of our relationships, our hopes, fears, and needs in such a way as to find something beyond the troubles and terrors of life—to find something worthy of our longing. Creativity pulls us out of the confinements and limitations of any given particular set of circumstances and expresses a "what if." And that "what if" captures the workings of imagination expressed through sets of skills, talents, and commitments. This, of course, is not to say all human creativity is noble or generative, nor appreciative of difference. Human creativity has nurtured expansive possibilities that pull us to be our best and others that urge us to demonize difference. Examples of both are noteworthy. Nonetheless, one thing is clear: An insular approach—for example, monologue—might provide food for thought for those who are in agreement with the speaker, but it offers little opportunity for complexity generated by having a range of opinions interact. Without conversation, little is done to promote a multidirectional and layered understanding of human expressive culture and what such production explains about the humans involved. Such is to say, this book's aims are relatively modest—to bracket debate over who is right—and instead, it looks at the work and aims of humans. And it does this by (1) privileging conversation as a more productive form of information sharing and (2) privileging the work of people as opposed to their ideological leanings. The intent in the following exchanges isn't to disprove or persuade but rather to think together.[20]

Mic Off: From Podcast to Book

Unlike many of the podcasts produced by Only Sky Media, "Pinn Drop" (from which these conversations are drawn) had a somewhat subtle engagement with humanism in part because I wanted to be in conversation with people holding to a range of orientations. Based on my personal orientation and much of my work, it's reasonable to assume something about this volume is meant as a framing of "secularism" in general and "Black secularism" in particular.[21] If we think about secularism as a shift in our social world by means of which it has become increasingly easy to think and interact outside of traditional theological grammars and vocabularies (e.g., God), then, yes, something about what these conversations entail suggests secularism. But, if what one means by secularism involves a more decidedly anti-religious orientation then, no, this isn't a project framed by secularism (Black or otherwise).[22] Continuing this line of thought, some contributors are critical of particular philosophical-theological orientations, and they speak to this; and others, through their personal commitments, implicitly select one orientation over others. Again, some of my conversation partners are atheists or humanists, and others are spiritual or theists. Yet, what undergirds this volume as a whole is an appreciation for the range of philosophical orientations (from atheism to theism) that shape how we, as humans, understand ourselves, ourselves in relationship to others, and ourselves in relationship to the world.

I picked these contributors because they are significant figures who offer—through their work and philosophy of life—a range of orientations moving from atheism to liberal theism. I asked myself a simple question: Who are some of the people doing really interesting work, and whose insights would make for good conversation, and would help to add complexity to our understanding of what it means to be meaning-making creatures? In a word, I wanted them to help me think about the human (that animated *human*ism *and* a host of other orientations). In most of the interviews, the concern with people trumps any particular *ism* used to establish the existential-ontological parameters of those people. What holds the ten conversations together, in a sense, is a basic concern to better understand the interests and capacities that undergird creative efforts. Some of these conversations involve a chat about what they have created personally, and in other cases it involves conversation about what they have chronicled, reflected on, or, in some way, have curated.

The discussions are arranged in two groups. The first ("Creatively Human") entails various takes on the nature and meaning of our humanity—giving expression to the psychological, social, and affective dimensions of what it means to be human and how we go about expressing the import of that humanity. The second part ("Human Creativity") presents ways in which human creativity gets conveyed through various outlets, including the arts and the sciences.[23]

In Part One, reflecting on the expansive sweep of human history, Candace Gorham, drawing from personal experience, thinks about how human creativity can undertake the business of helping nonbelievers mourn loss and heal from emotional and psychological harm. Coming out of an evangelical Christian context, Candace began to appreciate the need for ways to move through the world mindful of our human obligations and difficulties. As a humanist and an atheist, she recognized that nonbelievers often lack the tools and practices needed to address some of those human obligations as they revolve around getting through loss and depression. But, unlike many nontheists, Candace finds some value in religious language—for example, spirituality—for capturing affective concerns and possibilities that animate our lives. As she explains during our conversation, her book, *On Death, Dying and Disbelief*,[24] is meant to help humanists deal with issues of loss through some very personal stories and ten tips that encourage us to see the depth of our existence in relationship to others, and to find a vocabulary and set of practices that help us address and move through breaks in those relationships.

Nadya Dutchin—reflecting on her work over the years—talks about her efforts related to an expansive sense of love that urges access and justice for the marginalized. This sense of love and the action it conditions, for Nadya, is tied to humanist sensibilities. Still, according to Nadya, there is room in the effort for justice and access for people of various philosophical positions— theists and nontheists—as long as they prioritize transformative action that seeks greater inclusion.

I talk to Christopher Cameron about his book on Black secularism—*Black Freethinkers: A History of African American Secularism*.[25] We touch on why he wrote it, and the types of misconceptions regarding Black nonbelief he encountered in the literature he reviewed as part of his research. Christopher unpacks the rich history of Black nonbelief and the ways in which that philosophy of life was meant to produce a robust sense of personhood and humanity within a society saturated with anti-Black racism. He points out that disbelief isn't new to Black communities, but rather is part of the rich history of Black radical thought and the effort to reconstitute Black identity and personhood outside the negative framework of discrimination—all lodged within Black cultural production.

Reflecting on his life as an academic, secular humanist, and founding figure in Secular Studies, Phil Zuckerman explores his introduction to the study of sociology, and the manner in which it allowed him to address social structures in the world, and to do so through a secular lens. While advocating for a skeptical view of religion, he understands both personally and professionally the type of comfort secured from religiosity—and he isn't interested in taking that away, particularly in light of the fact that he has nothing better to offer. As he explains to me, the values he seeks to equip students with are empathy, an ability to hear differing opinions and respond in thoughtful and respectful ways, and a sense of empiricism. It is by means of these values that they are able to explore and get a better sense of what people believe (or don't believe) and what all of that means for collective life in our social world.

In Part II, Angelbert Metoyer describes becoming an artist, noting that he wouldn't have considered himself an artist until his thirties. Prior to that, he would have described himself in terms of whatever he was doing at the moment. As I come to learn, for Angelbert time is fluid, and this allows his work to move between past, present, and future without restriction. There are also ways in which how he engages the world—for example, family and community history and connections—inform and shape his art. He describes his work as layered, as transforming materials that are typically discarded. Angelbert's work seeks to transform objects, in the way a gardener reshapes conditions so as to allow a different reality.

Jamal Cyrus talks about the various influences on his work—from figures like John Biggers, to Harlem Renaissance artists. We discuss ways in which Jamal's work draws on the concept of disruption, but also collage, to produce pieces that draw from, unpack, and explore Black experience and history. In his art there is a creative tension between the spiritual and the political that he unpacks by drawing on sources such as West African ritual items and everyday materials like denim.

Using film as a means by which to understand history and culture, Jeremiah Camara discusses what he finds compelling and what he finds lacking in Black people's engagement with the sociopolitical and economic spheres of collective life. For him, these shortcomings, in part, stem from poor thinking and limited motivation that in certain ways originate in problematic ideologies. Through film, as he explains it, he seeks to highlight the harsh circumstances of life and encourage a thoughtful, and productive, response.

Harry Allen, one of the original commentators on Hip Hop culture, discusses the relationship of Hip Hop to identity formation and human values. He presses the point that Hip Hop is organic and that it grows out of particular contexts—shifts the dynamics of language and technology so as to tell alternate stories of life. Our conversation explores the moral and ethical framework suggested by Hip Hop culture as well as the ways in which it shifts and changes language in order to express the reality of those within the culture.

Valerie Cassel Oliver discusses the way in which much of her curatorial work has involved rendering visible the artists (and work) that have often been missing within the museum space. And these artists, Valerie reminds us, are citizens of the world who, in their work, respond to experience and encounters in that world. This may not involve complete narratives, complete social stories, but they are engagements with and responses to the world. The museum by extension serves to tell the stories of art but connected to important developments in our sociocultural worlds.

Finally, Philip Butler explains that for many people AI is scary in that they envision its potential to end human life. But for him there are other ways to think about AI and to maintain a more balanced work. This includes things like skewing toward marginalized communities and avoiding an uncritical reasserting of historical mores into AI models. To help guard against AI that simply reenforces our worst thinking and behaviors, he explains, we need to call for a distinction between humans and people—with the former a construct of the Enlightenment and the latter a more complex and local thing. Mindful of this, machines would need to be built that don't play off Enlightenment constructs that disadvantage and marginalize so many. Instead, we need to build machines that work from the vantage point of the localized, and in this way better address issues such as racism and sexism in AI.

The conversations that make up this volume are both disciplined and freewheeling. There is an overarching thematic structure—human creativity expressed in the form of music, the visual arts, writing, programming, ritual practices, organizing community building, and film—but the conversations liberally move across ideas. Again, they offer no final answers; but instead, it is our hope that they will inspire readers to start and keep conversations going. And in that way learn more about who we are, what we do, and why it all matters so much.

PART I

Creatively Human

1

Grieving While Disbelieving

Candace Gorham

Anthony: There are some folks that you just know you have to chop it up with, that you have to have a conversation with, but you don't get that opportunity often enough. Well, Candace Gorham is one of those folks for me. Our paths have crossed at various humanist and atheist conferences and gatherings, but we've never had a chance to say more than "what's up" and keep it moving. Candace has degrees from North Carolina Central University and Wake Forest University. She's a licensed professional counselor with a background in middle and high school education. And this work in high school education extends beyond the United States. But that's a different story. That's a different conversation. Candace's religious background covers a range of perspectives from Jehovah's Witnesses to Methodism. She's a former evangelical minister, entering ministry early. Her ministry included activities like casting out demons, and anyone who knows anything about evangelical ministry—or evangelical worship—knows that casting out demons is a big deal. As is a common story for those of us who leave theism, the failure of Christianity, for example, to address profound suffering, and the Bible's contradictions and moral and ethical shortcomings result in us having to get out. There were profound questions her faith couldn't answer. So, she left. Moving, as Candace describes it, from being an unaffiliated believer to being an atheist. Recognizing this story was shared by so many Black women, she founded (in 2013) the Ebony Exodus Project, which explores why Black women are leaving the church. She wrote a marvelous book by the same title. She's a member of the secular therapist project, and the clergy project. And she's the author of the recently published book *On Death, Dying and Disbelief*.[1]

Candace: Thank you for having me. And I'm so excited to be here, finally get a chance to sit down and talk to you. Yeah, this is fantastic.

Anthony: There's a whole lot I want to cover in our time together. But let me say this, in reading *On Death, Dying, and Disbelief*, one of the things that stood out for me is how deeply personal it is. You open your life to readers. And all of us who write books will argue that there's something of us in our books—something about them is autobiographical, but not quite like this. And one of the things that caught my attention was the way in which you marked out certain statements with a star, indicating, as you wrote, "This is where I cried." I had never encountered anything like this. In the book you say that you're writing it for two reasons. One, nontheists need this, they need to know how to deal with grief. And with that I give a secular "Amen." But you also say it was an opportunity to deal with your own grief. I have to believe that there's something about this book that's also tied to earlier life and earlier experiences, that there's something about this book that's also tied to your move from theism into what you label nontheism. Is that right?

Candace: Oh, yeah, and I will say, I guess you could argue that because the whole premise of the book is that we as nonbelievers, nontheists, atheists, humanists don't have the same resources to latch on to when we're grieving. I came out of a tradition where I had a plethora of resources in terms of prayer or support networks if I were grieving. Whereas now, as an atheist, as a nonbeliever, nontheist, I don't have those things. So, you could argue that I'm coming from a place of having had one experience. And now having a totally different experience dealing with grief.

Anthony: I don't think we can tell our stories of deconversion too often, or with too much energy. Folks need to hear that you can leave theism, develop a secular set of values. And you can survive the move. But I'd like to hear a bit more, if you're willing, concerning that transition. You weren't just in church. The Jehovah's Witnesses and evangelical Christianity, these are deep and all-consuming forms of religiosity. What about that departure? And how did that occur?

Candace: My dad was actually a Jehovah's Witness. And my mom was never really into it; she did it because her husband told her to do it—to be involved.[2] Even as a young child, I could tell that she wasn't really feeling it. My parents separated when I was nine or ten years old. And when my parents separated, immediately my mom said, "I'm not going back to the Kingdom Hall." But I, as a child, was really into my religion so I continued to do home study.

There was this family that came around every week, and I would go to the Kingdom Hall with them. Memorial services and Easter—they don't call it Easter, of course, you know—I would do all of those events with that family. Even as a child, I was way more serious about my religious beliefs and convictions and my religious practices than people around me, and my friends would always pick on me—like, "Yo, what are you? Let's go to the park man. It's time to play, and you over there trying to read the Bible, like what the hell." And so, when I got to middle school, I finally did drift away from the Jehovah's Witnesses, but only because I started going to a different church. And that's how I got into Methodism. My dad had grown up in the United Methodist Church. I started going to that church with my aunt and my cousins. I was confirmed in the Methodist tradition. I was in the choir, the children's choir, and I did all of that stuff, and was baptized. I went through all of those processes there.

I got to high school and got a job, got a boyfriend—all the things you do when you go to high school and you get a boyfriend. I drifted away from church a little bit. Then my senior year in high school, my sister married a pastor, and that's when things started to get interesting. She married this pastor, and I decided that I wanted to follow my sister down the path that she was going down. He was the one who brought more extreme religious practices into our lives, and he was the one that was into the casting out of demons and praying for seven to ten days at a time, street evangelism, prophesying. I joke, but yeah, I'm always telling people I can still prophesy: $10 and I tell you whatever you want to hear!

I got into extreme religious practices, got married, and my husband was into it as well. I started going through some things, and we were able to break away from that church specifically because my sister and her husband moved to California. We started going to another church that was a mega-church, a prosperity Gospel Church. You had to give your tithes and offerings. And you had to give a second offering, and a third . . . that type of church. One of the pastor's favorite lines was, "if you're not living like me, you're doing something wrong." His wife drove a Mercedes and he drove a Harley, and they lived in a gated community. They didn't release the financials of the church, but he was clearly living a prosperous life. And people internalized his message: "if you're not living like me, you're doing something wrong." I really did believe I was doing something wrong because my house went into foreclosure, I lost a car, and I was severely depressed. I was really going through a tough time in my life. I thought, am I seriously doing something wrong? What am I doing wrong? Let me pray some more. I started studying harder and looking at new texts and considering new things and new ways of thinking about Christianity, about God and religion. And I studied myself right on out of religion! I like to tell people it wasn't an emotional decision. I wasn't angry at God. It was a purely intellectual process.

Anthony: You know, we share Methodism—for you, United Methodism, and for me the African Methodist Episcopal Church. My church wasn't the typical AME Church; it was much more evangelical, concerned with the gifts of the Spirit. Speaking in tongues, dancing in the spirit, casting out demons. That life was all consuming.

And growing up in that church family, I did not have the ability to distinguish myself. My sense of identity—who I was—was intimately connected to the church. I described myself and I thought about myself using the vocabulary and grammar of that church. I could not detangle myself. Like you, I moved into ministry, and I'm certain we shared a sense of what constitutes a productive ministry: Are folks finding Jesus? Are folks getting saved? Are demons being cast out? Are folks growing in their knowledge of the Lord?

I think our movement out of the Christian church was also somewhat similar. I think our story is the typical story. And that makes a lot of sense. For me, it was the inability to explain the world; it was the inability to offer anything that really spoke to the well-being of the folks I cared about. I didn't have anything in my theological bag that allowed me to speak to well-being in a way that appreciated embodied human life. And it reached a point for both of us where we had to make a decision. Am I about safeguarding this tradition? Or, am I about speaking the truth to the human condition? What am I willing to give up to be able to speak honestly about the human condition? You left. I left.

It seems to me within our shared religious experience, we were given a set of values meant to guide how we move through the world. And I'm curious, what of those values did you leave behind? And which of those values did you take with you?

Candace: What values did I leave behind? I think I left behind things that were judgmental—stuff that had to do with beliefs about who's gonna go to heaven and who's gonna go to hell. What makes you a good person, what makes you a bad person—that you can just sort of live, you can live a crappy life, right? And then just pray on your deathbed, and you're good to go in the "sweet by and by." Back then I didn't think I was a judgmental person. I thought: oh, I'm living in the love of the Lord. That's all I was trying to share—the word of God.

I did go through a period of time when I had a lot of guilt, and I had a lot of shame inside me about ways that I was judgmental and mistreated people. I know that I hurt people by doing what I thought was the right thing. Now stuff that I really value are things like autonomy, personal choice—as long as you're not hurting people—living a good life. And that type of life involves making your own meaning, and not depending on some sort of external definition.

My humanist identity is really important to me. Obviously, I identify as an atheist; but the humanist side of me is really important. And it's because of that centering that I understand we're all we have, and we got to take care of each other. When I was a Christian, I paid lip service to the idea of taking care of each other. It was all about Jesus, right? It was all about God and saving souls for Jesus. Now, for me there's no attention to Jesus determining how I treat people and why I treat people a certain way.

Anthony: I think one of the things I had to come to grips with when I left the church was the degree to which the values I had embraced were opposed to life. This is what I mean by that: the values were so oriented toward the soul getting into heaven. And they positioned me to be so suspicious of this material world that I did not have a way to really appreciate embodied life, within the context of human history. That stuff wasn't what was important. This world was just what we had to go through to get to what was important. It was a bit of a challenge to move from that theologically formed system of values, to a secular system of values that was all about how you produce well-being for embodied bodies within the context of human history. This move to secular values entailed a sense of vulnerability that Tony Pinn, the Christian minister, didn't have to face because God was on the throne and all was well. But this secular set of values is still about fostering life; it's about love. It's about proper conduct. It's about deep respect, and it is solely reliant on us. So, you and I came to a conclusion that this theism doesn't work, that it's not substantive enough to move us through the world we love. Why do you think so many Black folks stay within religious organizations? And I ask that not as an accusation, but as a matter of genuine curiosity that pulls from your Ebony Exodus Project, and the interviews you conducted with respect to folks leaving. Why do you think so many remain in churches?

Candace: I think there's a couple of layers to that. I think that there's this psychological part, right? Darrel Ray[3] talks about the God virus and how it takes over psychologically—overriding our critical thinking skills. Religion takes a hold of our fears, and it controls us through those mechanisms. And then I think for Black people, it has historically been so rough that a reward in the afterlife is appealing, right? Jim Crow was hard; reconstruction was hard. These periods of time are really hard, and we know it. We're gonna suffer through this American life right now, but our reward is in the afterlife. Whatever you can latch on to that gives you some sense of peace that creates a trauma bond with religion. So, we've got fear; you've got the god virus; you've got all those things that are already at play for any human; then, you add on top of that our traumatic history and our trauma bond. It just becomes a kind of repeating pattern, like a generational curse. But, religion itself is the generational curse.

Anthony: Trauma bond. I've never heard that before. I'm gonna have to remember that. I need to write that down. I think it's important that we keep it real. I appreciate and I agree with everything you've said. I also think—particularly when white humanists and atheists fail to recognize the ways in which humanism and atheism, in the context of United States, have not been very welcoming—getting rid of God doesn't mean you get rid of your racism, your sexism, homophobia, and so on. I think, and let's chat about this a bit, that some remain in the church, despite the theology, for the sake of networking and community. If nothing else, this is a place where you don't have to explain why you're angry. It's a place where you don't have to worry about folks coming to you uninvited, and touching your hair. It's a place where you don't have to worry about folks coming up to you and saying, "you know, you're not like the others". The Black Church gets a whole lot wrong. It has never gotten gender, right. Forget about sexuality, but it has been a space away from the larger connotations and consequences of white nonsense. And it seems to me that until humanist organizations and humanist communities provide a soft space to land, Black folks, whether they are theist or not, will find something useful in churches.

Candace: No, you're absolutely right. We can't pretend that the Black Church has not provided positive benefit to the Black community at various times, in one way or another. In some of my interviews that I've done in the past, people have definitely said they feel like they get something positive out of it, like community. I get that. I have a friend right now who's a nonbeliever, but every now and then he just finds himself drawn to go to a church, because he can't seem to find a secular community around him that he feels comfortable in. And so, he has this incredible sense of loneliness. And what he remembers is that church gave him a sense of belonging. It's almost like a drug, like when I hear him talk about it, it sounds almost like somebody craving a drug. I can get the fix if I go to church. And then he's like, "but I know it's no good. It's just gonna hurt me, but I really want to go." I definitely know people, and I've done interviews with people, and they say exactly what you're saying. They don't believe all of what they're hearing or what they're being taught, but they do get something from church, so they continue to go.

Anthony: I think it's important to remember that churches are also businesses. During the civil rights movement, for example, the value of the church wasn't prayer or God. The value of the church during the movement was its physical space where folks could gather and strategize. The value of the church was its ability to allow for networking to get information out "quick, fast, and in a hurry". And again, until humanists develop comparable communities that constitute a soft place to land, folks are going to get what they need elsewhere and, in the process, put up with a whole lot of abuse for the sake of that network. What they need is a place to catch their breath. We humanists and atheists ought to be doing a better job of providing that.

Candace: Yeah, no, it's true. The numbers are definitely growing, and the demand is there for sure.

Anthony: One of the things I find really, really interesting about your new book—*On Death, Dying, and Disbelief*—is your perspective on the religious right—that there's often a tendency within humanist and atheist circles to simply belittle the religious. If a religious person happens to communicate with you using their theology and theological vocabulary, they're gonna catch a verbal beatdown, right? The religious person says, "God bless you," and they will catch a verbal beatdown. You provide a different perspective on this—the idea that when a religious person uses that language, uses those phrases, they're simply trying to demonstrate care using what's available to them. Can you say a bit more about that? I just found that so very interesting. So very appealing.

Candace: Yes, so when you are grieving, you are at the bottom of the barrel. You have minimal energy; you have minimal life in you. I mean, you're just really at the bottom. And part of the point that I make is you just don't use your precious resources to battle with somebody because they say "God bless you" when you sneeze. Or, to battle with them if they say "Can I pray with you?" You could, if you want to, say no thank you, but I don't see the point of going into a tirade behind that sort of thing. I make the point in the book that the majority of people in this country probably hold some sort of a religious belief. The majority of people are going to hold some sort of belief in an afterlife or something like that. So, you can just assume that if you tell somebody that you're grieving the loss of somebody, nine times out of ten, or six times out of ten, or whatever, whoever you're talking to is probably going to have some kind of religious or spiritual framework they use when approaching you. And so, when you already are struggling just to get out of the bed and go to work in the morning, or go to school in the morning, why fight a fight you're not going to win. So, I just say, they're giving you the only thing that they can think of that they have. Grief is such an ugly, scary, lonely thing. If somebody is trying to give you the only thing that they can think of, I just don't see the point in responding out of anger in that moment. Like I say in the book, if they're approaching you like that because they know you're an atheist, and they're trying to use this as an opportunity to get at you, then fine, give it to them! But, if they're coming at you because that's all that they know how to give you, then why? Why turn this into an ugly moment?

Anthony: And Candace, you say that you wrote this book, and I think this is absolutely true, because there are so few resources on grieving for nontheists. I need you to help me wrap my mind around this: you say that you use the category of nontheist for a variety of reasons—one being because of the spiritual dimensions associated with it. Help me understand what you're getting at.

Candace: I kind of struggled with that a little bit. I just felt like it was a little bit more of a generic term. It's not laden with as many heavy connotations as is "atheists." So, it's a little gentler of a word when the topic is so heavy already. I didn't want the discussion to be around language, you know, that's being used. And so, that was kind of what I was going for—to take the focus off of language when the audience I'm speaking to knows who I'm speaking to. It's a way to soften the language to a certain extent.

Anthony: You also rescue and recast some other vocabulary that we typically associate with theists—like ritual. You talk about the importance of ritual. Within the context of humanists and atheists, there are a whole lot of folks who are like, "Nah, I'm not with that." They assume ritual is for the theists. Why do you think it's so very important for grieving nontheists to appreciate and form ritual?

Candace: Rituals (and performing rituals) are something that the research shows humans have been doing since we've been human—since we've been Homo sapiens. We've been doing rich rituals of various kinds, right, for religious reasons, spiritual reasons, to get the sun to come up. And yeah, we've been doing rituals for every kind of reason—like to mark occasions to have babies—and so we do rituals all the time. You know, we don't realize that we do rituals, and we don't call them rituals. I think it's a satisfying thing to have something that's a standardized thing—something you can look forward to. This is especially true with grief and death—especially if it's unexpected, but I believe it can happen even when it is expected because you are never really prepared for loss. To develop some sort of a ritual that gives you a sense of predictability, gives you a sense of standardization, something tangible is important. I'm going to, you know, go to the grave, and I'm putting flowers there, and I'm going to do that every first Sunday of the month. This practice is standard and stable. There's just something I think that happens to us as humans when we have something predictable in our life.

Anthony: So, I wouldn't dare try to tell you what you're saying, but humor me. This is what I think I hear you saying: under all of this is the idea that nontheists have surrendered too much to theists. We've given away more than we need to give away. And as a result, we have cheated ourselves out of the ability to be creative, imaginative, and poetic with respect to our relationships. One of the things that you want nontheists to wrestle back into their sense of self and their sense of community is ritual. Right? There are folks in ritual studies who argue that ritual is simply repeated activity in founded space. And, whether humanists and atheists want to recognize it or not, they do ritual. Anytime they get together, at a conference or some other regularized meeting and do the same sort of stuff, greet folks in the same sort of way, they are doing rituals. That's ritual. I think you are just being wonderfully intentional concerning our use of ritual and bringing it into an area where humanists and atheists are typically rather clumsy and awkward—how to deal with loss, how to mourn.

Candace: You said that way better than I said it. That's perfect. And I think I love the way you say that we need to sort of rescue some of this language and boldly reclaim it, and feel comfortable using it in our own way. It kind of makes me think of the Black nonbelievers' cruise. I've been to three of the four, and every year I would consider what rituals we should include. For example, on the last night, at dinner, we do a shot. And then we always get a bottle of wine in our room. We all go out on the deck on the last night, and we sit around and we drink the bottles. We do this every year, you know—at the same time, at the same place. We absolutely do ritualistic-type things all the time that we don't even think about. We don't even call them that.

Anthony: Yeah. And here I think is the difference between nontheistic ritual and theistic ritual. Theistic ritual is meant to make us less human. That is to say, it's meant to highlight the God in us, to subdue the material human. Whereas nontheistic ritual is meant to enliven and celebrate our humaneness. Right? Theistic ritual is vertical in nature because it's meant to urge us to look beyond our earthly social engagement, but not for us to understand and appreciate more fully the way we interact with other folks and within the larger context of life.

One other thing I find extremely valuable and thought provoking about your book is the way in which you talk about nature as sanctuary. You hike, and that's all throughout this book. And there are ways in which hiking moves your story along, and it kind of moves us through the book. Can you say a bit more concerning nature as sanctuary?

Candace: So, I talked about what believers have, and I think I mentioned sanctuaries or cathedrals or something like that. And I say: but we nonbelievers have all the great outdoors, right? We have beautiful nature. That is our sanctuary; that is where we can go to rejuvenate and learn and grow. I talk in the book about research on Directed Attention Fatigue, and I talk about how we lose our ability to focus and make decisions.[4] We become grumpy and irritable when we don't spend enough time in nature, when we don't spend enough time engaging in activities that just allow us to shut down those certain areas of our brain that are constantly on. And the best way to kind of shut down those areas of our brain is to just get back outside, to get back in nature. I'm out there. Yeah, I'm out there at least once a week. I try to hike every Sunday, if I can. But I also understand people, if they live in a city, may not be able to do that. I can be in the mountains in two hours; I can be at the beach in two hours. Not everybody is able to do that. So, if all you can do is go sit on a park bench, then go sit on a park bench. If all you can do is sit on your front porch, during a rainstorm, sit on your front porch during a rainstorm. Just let yourself get back in touch with nature, appreciate the beauty of what's going on around you. And really focus on that. There are obvious things like the circle of life, you know, which helps you stay in touch as everything is born and everything dies. But there's something I think that happens to us, on a physiological level, when we're outside in a very natural element. I think it makes a huge difference when, for example, you're grieving. The research shows that it makes a big difference to our mental health and our physical health. And so, I try to make a big push in the book to highlight the research around how being outside is so good for us physically, mentally, and emotionally. Nonbelievers don't have cathedrals; we don't have sanctuaries. So, let's go outside. Let's do it. Let's do it our way.

Anthony: In terms of grieving, you provide ten tips. And the book really revolves around those ten tips—things nontheists ought to be thinking and doing as they move through grief. What would you label one or two things that nontheists typically get wrong with respect to grief?

Candace: What would I say they get wrong? I think one thing is what we talked about already—they misdirect energy. They focus on arguing with people about God, get into discussions about whether a person is in heaven or hell, or get into discussions with family about the beliefs or nonbelief of the deceased person. Or they misdirect energy by getting into arguments about religion in general. I think people's buttons get pushed a little bit more because everybody's around, and everybody's talking about religion. People end up getting into debates and discussions and arguments around religion. When you're grieving, I don't recommend burning your energy on that. I think that people also neglect their mental health. I think people just write it off as grief, but they don't recognize the value of getting some professional support during that time. Even though it is grief, and maybe you're not clinically depressed, you're not developing schizophrenia, and it's not pathological doesn't mean you would not benefit from professional support. So, I think a lot of people miss that, but professional support could really go a long way toward making the situation less unpleasant.

Anthony: Could you talk a bit about the ten tips? How did you come up with them? What is the basic takeaway of these tips?

Candace: The way I came up with the ten—well, some of them were just things that helped me, such as reconnecting with nature. That's just plain and simple. I knew immediately there would be a chapter talking about nature. I'm a licensed professional counselor, so I knew off the bat there would be a chapter talking about mental health. Some of that was just because of my personal experience and my professional expertise. And then some of those tips, like the first one, come from questions that people have asked me about the supernatural. Wow, I can't think of how it's worded right now. But basically, I'm sort of like normalizing the fact that you may have things that look like supernatural experiences, and it's okay. And the tenth tip is more for somebody who's just trying to support somebody who's grieving. They are really practical things, like what we can do to help somebody who's grieving. And that was just me reflecting on what would have helped me. I also talked to other people who were grieving and got input from them—what was helping them, and what was important to them. It's kind of a crowdsource list of what people say helped them.

Anthony: I'm struggling here a bit because I don't want to say too much. People need to read the book. And our conversation should not replace reading the book. So, again, I'm struggling a little bit. So, I'm going to confine my energy and my thinking, and ask you to just pick one of the general practices, the tips, and drill down just a little bit.

Candace: Let's see. Okay, so we talked about the tip concerning spending time in nature. There's a study that shows heart patients benefit from exposure to nature. In the study, the ones who had windows in their rooms facing outdoors had better outcomes; they use less pain medicine, and they recover faster. Some heart surgery patients, rather than windows were given photographs. Those people who had nature scenes (windows or photographs) versus those who did not had better outcomes. In terms of Directed Attention Fatigue and Restoration Therapy, I try to use research and really try to drill down deeply in that chapter because I know, I'm biased, right?[5] Another chapter that I really like is the chapter on crying, and the benefits of crying—different chemicals that our body's producing, or the ways that the parasympathetic nervous system is stimulated, or endogenous opioids are released. All these things we're learning about the body, and the ways that the body responds when we cry. And I always try to make sure that I include meaningful research in addition to the personal stories, the journals, and poems. I hope that people will pay attention to the research because that is the foundation to me. I'm very serious about science and research and making sure that we're not just saying stuff. There's got to be evidence, evidence-based support, for the decisions we make and the things that we're doing.

Anthony: At the very beginning of the book, you talk in terms of the historical moment and folks living through the COVID pandemic also being part of the motivation for writing. I'm wondering if we can talk about grief, loss, and mourning in relation to the dynamics of the United States. I think we both recognize how anti-Black this nation is. And so, Black folks are living within the context of a social world that is defined by anti-Blackness, and death-dealing circumstances, including COVID. In a real way, to be Black and alive is to be well aware of death—the constant threat of death. Right? We are constantly bombarded with the potential for demise. And so, how do these tips work in relation to the general sense of grief, of loss, of mourning, of death, that Black life entails in the United States?

Candace: Oh, man, you know, that's such a good point. We are perpetually aware, right, that our lives are at risk, that our lives (our bodies) are not safe. Just to take a quick second, before I answer your question, this weekend was my daughter's birthday. We love nature, so we were in a little cabin in the mountains of Tennessee. It's just me and my sister. We took all of our children—my one daughter, my sister's children, and my brother's children. These two women and a bunch of kids! Here we are, in two trucks driving through the winding roads of the Tennessee mountains and paths—Trump signs and rebel flags everywhere. The whole ride, like the whole ride, three and a half hours like this: No, we're not gonna stop at this gas station. Candace, you got your gun? Yes, I have my gun. This perpetual fear of just trying to get them to a cabin in the woods—this perpetual fear of what is going to happen. I understand what you're saying about anti-Blackness—the stress and the sense of general loss.

I think that the book is valuable to believers, to nonbelievers—and all forms of grief, death, losing a job, losing a dog. Because the tips themselves are about good stress management, life management tips, you know, things like getting sleep, taking your medicine, calling on help when you need help, not getting into unnecessary arguments. The stuff that I'm saying is good life management, stress management, mental health, physical health management, tips. And so, I think that they absolutely can be applied to all kinds of situations and all kinds of scenarios—including normal, everyday chronic stress that Black Americans face.

Anthony: As I was reading your book, this phrase kept echoing in my head from Thoreau's *Walden*—live deliberately, so that at the end you know you have lived.[6] I'm paraphrasing, but that's the general idea. It kept coming back to me in relation to the tips as a way to kind of think about living deliberately. So, in terms of crying, for example, it's encouragement to live deliberately on one level because it encourages us to be aware of ourselves, to be aware of how the world touches our embodied selves. And I just found that powerful. I also kept thinking as I was reading that the circumstances are different for Black people—whether a theist or a nontheist. Black people have to teach their children how not to die.

Candace: That's right. Black people have to teach their children how not to die.

Anthony: That's different than being able to teach your children to be curious, to be imaginative, to touch the world and be touched by the world. For us the touch of the world can be deadly. We have to teach our children how not to die. And so, I would agree with you that there are ways in which the tips you provide work for us, regardless of our particular life circumstances. They work for us because we live in the context of a social world that is death dealing.

Candace: Yeah, very good. Very good. Absolutely. I think you're making a great point—saying we live in a world that is death dealing. It's unfortunate to have to say that we teach our children how not to die. Even in the best of circumstances, we still have to teach our children how not to die. And that's just such a powerful phrase, right?

Anthony: And how does that not weigh on you? How does that not weigh on you in a way that has physical, emotional, psychological, affective consequences? How does it weigh on those children? I think you're right; we have not been conditioned; we've not been taught how to deal with the impact of that stress.

Candace: Well, what we have been taught to do is to pray, to go read your Bible. That's the only strategy we've been given. We haven't been given any other strategies.

Anthony: And there's a problem with that strategy, right? The Christian tradition is dependent upon suffering. The major marker for that tradition is the Christ event—the cross, the crucifixion, and the resurrection. It is a tradition that is built upon the usefulness of suffering. How can that tradition then teach you how to deal with loss when loss is a problem and not a benefit? And add to that dilemma the death-dealing consequences of anti-Black racism?

How does that tradition and those privileges celebrate suffering, and teach you to move beyond suffering? That's a tall order.

Candace: Yeah, no, exactly. Exactly.

Anthony: That's a rough one. In your book, you say acceptance is not about being okay with loss. It's about allowing the loss to be a part of your life in a different way. Help me understand that.

Candace: That's really difficult to discuss. When I think about my loved one, and losing him. For me it has been about him still being with me on a daily basis. You know, it's been two and a half years. And I think about him daily. I still talk about him on a regular basis. I had a whole episode about him just the other day on the phone talking about him. And so, I think he's incorporated in my life in a different way. Now, because I've written this book, and I talk about him and cry about him at conferences in front of people, he's still very much with me but in a different way. I continue to celebrate him, and I continue to memorialize him daily. I'm never gonna be okay, you know, with him not being here. But I'm much better than I was a year ago, two years ago. I have a way to deal with it and I have a way to incorporate it in my life that is helping me to deal with it in a constructive way. A lot of people would try to sort of sweep it under the rug, don't talk about it anymore, lock the kid's bedroom, and leave it just like it was the day the child left. Never touch that bedroom again, or whatever. Never unpack your husband's closet or whatever, right? They just kind of let things freeze in time, and not deal with it. The healthy thing is to figure out a way to continue to celebrate that person, remember that person, and talk about that person—let that person be a part of your life. Even though they're not there physically, how can they continue to be a part of your life?

Anthony: You say in the book that a conversation about relationships, romantic and otherwise, could be a whole other book. I'm curious. What would you say in this other book about nontheistic relationships and nontheistic community? Just a preview of that book, what would you say?

Candace: Well, I think when I say that, it wasn't necessarily that I was thinking about, like, the religious side of it. I was just thinking about more specifically trying to start relationships again with that much grief. So, full transparency, that's kind of what I was breaking down about the other day, I kind of have a little romantic interest right now. And that's where my breakdown was coming from. I'm not sure that I can go in this direction because of still having so much grief. I don't know, I can't answer. Maybe there'll be a book, we'll see.

But I was thinking more along the lines of the struggle with moving forward in a romantic way, when you've lost a romantic lover or partner. So, we'll see.

Anthony: And is there a way then, to kind of think about that in terms of just intimacy? How to establish intimacy after this kind of loss?

Candace: Yeah, we always talk about communication being key, right? I think that is a big deal. I think that there has to be that communication. It's significant. And so, you've got to be comfortable with really communicating openly with that person. And that person has to be comfortable with you—with the fact that you may still be mourning a love. Is your new lover going to be okay with the fact that you're still mourning an old lover? You know, are they going to be comfortable? Hey, we may be in the middle of an intimate act, and I'm breaking down crying about an old lover. So, there's a lot of communication that's going to have to go on around that. We've got baggage from all relationships. It may just happen to be death, but it is still baggage impacting a new relationship. It has to be dealt with; you got to deal with it personally. And some of it may have to be dealt with in connection to that new potential partner because it's an interpersonal thing.

Anthony: You've been really generous with your time, so one last question. The book really deals with how individuals might move through grief, what we ought to understand about grieving, and how we move through this process in a way that respects who we are, what we are, and where we are. I'm wondering if there is something you would say to the humanist community writ large. Let's think in terms of all of the major organizations, what should be the takeaway for those organizations with respect to these issues of loss, and grief, and mourning? What should the movement be doing differently and better?

Candace: I would say that the takeaway is we need resources. We need resources—training humanist celebrants to be available to provide ceremonies, funds for writers so that they can sit down and create content for us. The large organizations that have the money can help back some of these projects to create content that's needed. And like we talked about earlier, we need soft places to land, and more of the discussions people are hungry for.

2

When to Walk, When to Fight

Nadya Dutchin

Anthony: Today, I have the pleasure of talking with Nadya Dutchin—a proud alumna of Florida A&M University, with a degree in molecular and cellular biology. She's is executive director of ShareBaby, and prior to that Nadya was executive director of the American Humanist Association.[1] She currently serves on the Board of the Common Good Generation, which is committed to justice through organizing toward possibilities where those more impacted by structural inequalities are centered. Common Good Generation believes conditions which result in the freedom of those most impacted by structural inequalities liberate us all. Nadya is the treasurer of the Baltimore Green Justice Workers Cooperative and a board member of the Nonprofit Industrial Complex (a secular mutual aid organization). And that's not all, she's also board president of Our Climate Education Fund, which empowers young people to advocate for climate justice policies that build a thriving world by engaging and training young people from affected communities and groups to participate in broad and diverse advocacy coalitions.[2] Thanks for hanging out with me.

Nadya: Thank you so much for having me, Anthony. I'm so excited to talk with you.

Anthony: Your entire professional career you have been involved in social justice. I'm wondering what sparked that interest? Was there something about your time at Florida A&M University[3] that led to this commitment?

Nadya: I think it's about social justice *and* equal access. Those are the things that have driven me because I was in health care nonprofit for a long time. And what brought me to that is my first job out of college—working for the phone company in a call center. It was the worst. I met lovely people there. I think I treated the customers well, and it was a good experience. I learned sales, which gave me a springboard to jump into some other things. But I did not want to work for corporate interests. It really solidified that I wanted to leave the world a better place than I found it. So, I was really committed at that point. Once I left that, I was mostly committed to working for nonprofit organizations to make the world a better place.

Anthony: Fantastic! I heard you say in an interview that the first time you heard of humanism was a few years ago, but it seems like something about humanism captures your philosophy of life. Could you tell me a bit about your philosophy of life—how it developed, and how you reached your current state of freethought?

Nadya: One of things I'm really good at is loving people. And I always said to myself that if I could work in a job and just love people, give people love, and make them feel comfort, joy, and satisfaction, that's what I would do. And that's the way I see this work as standing in, as rooted in love to affect change. There's a tide right now, and we need to ride that tide. We need to get on our surfboards and ride the wave. There's such a need. I think we've come to the clear end of unfettered capitalism that is just greedy, rapacious, unyielding, unwieldy, unseemly, unkind. And people are tired of it. In this moment, I think humanism is the place where we can stand literally looking to alleviate the suffering of people. And nobody can do that better. Not the government, not our politicians, as much as we need them to codify good policy. Who will save us will be us. The last couple of years of COVID showed us that when we need one another, we show up. And it didn't feel like that going in. I think I felt dread going into COVID. I was like, oh my gosh, people are gonna eat each other alive in their homes, and people are gonna take to the streets. And I saw something totally different, and it really renewed my faith in people. So, now coming to the American Humanist Association, and coming to this place when I have always, unknowingly, identified as a humanist—I didn't know that is what it was called. But now coming into this place, where all of the professional skills that I have, all of the places that I've organized and I've worked, my passion for resourcing and supporting young people is actually coming together, and I can put it to good use in one place. Right now, what we need is policy and action that's rooted in love. I get to do that; I get to stand in my purpose, and it's the first time in a very, very long time that I've felt this way.

Anthony: I think you're very generous in terms of how you describe the humanist community. I think there are a lot of folks who can get with what you're saying. But there are other folks who have a rather narrow sense of what justice entails. They have a narrow sense of compassion. So, for example, I've heard this more than once concerning Black Christians: "Look, if they want to believe that stuff, they deserve whatever happens to them!" I don't hear the love in that. So, I get how we do this in terms of the likeminded, but what do we do with those within humanist circles for whom this expansive sense of access and justice is a challenge? In humanist circles, at least the humanist circles in which I'm involved, I don't hear love as the anchor very often. I hear community. I hear science education. I hear separation of church and state, but I don't often hear love as the anchor. Can you just say a bit more concerning what you mean by love as the anchor, the motivation for humanist work?

Nadya: So first, I'd like to push back a little bit concerning that first point you made, particularly with respect to the Black Church, which we know is toxic. And I think it's for that reason that some of us throw our hands up because you can't argue with people who are brainwashed. You can't argue with them until they are willing to open up their eyes and their hearts, and continue to ask questions beyond their cognitive dissonance. Trying to have conversations with them is tiring; it's like hitting your head against the wall. And it's demoralizing. I think we can invite people into the space who are religious and who maybe humanist unbeknownst to them. I think a lot of people who are spiritual or religious feel the same way—for these folks, there are commonalities that go unnoticed: Aren't you a good person? Don't you like people? Don't you care about the condition of people? Don't you believe in science? Well, then, you're a humanist. Welcome to the movement! We know what we know, and they know what they know. There's no space for that, but we can serve together. But that is the opportunity we have. There's some shallowness in, not just the Black Church, but the church in general—a lot of prosperity gospel, a lot of pontificating, a lot of looking down their noses at people. And not a whole lot of service. Paying tithes determines what type of treatment you get in the church. We don't see them opening the doors of their church for people to sleep when it's cold, or opening their kitchens to feed people. There are plenty of organizations and churches that do that work, but we don't see a lot of that. But can we serve together? And we can. Many hands make light work, and if we are working the way we need to and as diligent as we need to, we can simply appreciate that human experience together. That's the bridge that we build between us. But it is difficult to be around folks who are toxic to you. For especially Black folks, Diaspora religion is often the anchor for the family, and when you walk away from that, and say you don't believe in God anymore, they're like, you're a terrible person. It's hard to be around those people. And people in the humanist movement need to protect their peace. If you need to divorce yourself from those communities until you're in a better place—when you've gotten out of acute trauma from being in the church, then maybe you can go back and work with them. But I wouldn't recommend it because it isn't healthy. We don't need to deal with toxicity just to make a point.

Anthony: I would agree with you, but let's stay on this point for a minute because it's important. The situation is complex. As a fellow humanist, I would agree with you concerning what often takes place in Christian circles, but it doesn't capture the thought or work of a Senator Raphael Warnock, or a Freddie Haynes, or a Vashti McKenzie.[4] There are those within the context of Christianity who are trying to rethink it. So, one of the questions for me is, as humanists, how do we decipher these differences, these nuances, so that we can work in solidarity with those who are committed to the same sense of justice and access—while still being critical of members of their larger theological organizations who don't share that commitment to justice and access? And on a related note, I'm with you on this issue of toxicity and moving away from. But regarding even Christians who are ass backward, do they deserve the injustice they encounter?

Nadya: Oh, no. And you pointed out great people. Rev. William Barber of the Poor People's Campaign[5] is another example. Again, that's the work, that's the serving, and we can do that together. But whether they want to work with us is a whole different situation. Because I say it all the time, I think people think that we humanists murder chickens and babies in our backyards. I don't know what they think of those, those of us that are godless. And I don't know that they think we're good people. But that's where conversation and breaking bread come into play—sitting down and having conversations and finding those commonalities together. I think around the world, people of the global majority, which is all brown and Black people, have more in common (even with white people) than different. And I think we need to lean into those similarities. It doesn't matter how we get there because I believe in decentralized networks. It doesn't matter if one movement is running, one is on skates, one is on a speedboat, while some folks are crawling. It doesn't matter how we get there. We can use different tactics to get to equity, to get to actual justice. We can get there together. We may get there at different times, and we may do it in different ways, but we have got to learn to be in a place of respect. And it is really difficult when you're dealing with people—particularly Black folk—who are dealing with acute trauma from being in the church. It's real, real hard to dig deep and find compassion for people who continue to allow themselves to be in a position of abuse. If something is horrible, it's horrible. Right? And we can agree on that and take action together.

Anthony: You've talked in terms of love, but what are some of the other values that you think are inherent to humanism, that we ought to be communicating to the larger public?

Nadya: I think empathy is something that I'm seeing in short supply, even in our own humanist movement, which has been a bit disappointing honestly. I've been in meetings with people who have been in and have led our movement for decades—probably even decades before I was born—and who have used language like "woke" and "social justice warrior." And they've said the movement is now "too woke," "too progressive." I'm like, when did we stop wanting to be progressive? Isn't that the point of progress, to progress? We don't want to move on and grow? But we deserve better, our children and our children's children deserve better. In sales training, that horrible job that I had, one of the most important things that I learned is when to walk away. And that ain't easy. It's real hard, but you can press the sale so many times, but at some point you have to be like—you know what, this opportunity cost is not worth it! You're making me sweat and be uncomfortable. This is not working. So, thank you—have a great day, take care of yourself, and move on. I'm in that place with some folks in our movement, who may not necessarily have the energy—and I recognize that it may simply be a matter of like energy and not having the capacity to learn something else. I think as we get older, we get a little bit rigid. I think we can get rigid in our thinking and rigid in our acceptance of new and different ideas. But, if this movement is going to survive, we have to be flexible, limber, and agile. We have to be proactive and not reactive. And I think there's been a lot of reactivity in this movement. I think that baton passing and legacy planning, succession planning is actually important. And I don't want us to just cast away folks who don't necessarily want to go out and work with a social justice organization in their community, or even give us their money anymore. There's room for them to do something in the movement, and maybe it's simply to pass on knowledge. It's a little disappointing at times, but I want our movement to be welcoming to people—not *feel* welcoming but *be* welcoming. And that means everyone. We've got to decolonize the way that we think about movements and how we think about our place in them, everyone's place in them. I'm here to upend all of that—proudly, excitedly, happily, there's a lot of changes coming, and some people are not going to be okay with it. There have been other organizations in the secular movement where they can go, but we're going to work. So, again, if we're standing in love, in compassion and respect for folks with empathy, understanding other people's condition, it doesn't matter how you got there. It's not my job to stand in judgment. That's why we left the church in order to step out of judgment. My job is not to judge you. My job is to help make your life better. It's the empathy that I think is missing from some of our "seasoned crowd." I don't think they can wrap their minds around just how free people are, and that's the point, we want to be liberated.

Anthony: I'm with you in terms of where the humanist movement needs to go, but I'm wondering if getting there requires major changes to our infrastructure and our models of leadership. And, if that is the case, what kinds of changes need to happen?

Nadya: Yeah, absolutely. I think there are some severe structural changes that need to happen in our movement. And I'm thinking about them. I'm thinking about what they can look like. And I don't know, to be perfectly honest with you. I'm just getting to the place where I'm able to start looking at our American Humanist Association chapters and our members and how we engage with one another, our partnerships, which are so incredibly key, and how we're investing in young people. I feel very supported, knowing that nobody expects me to snap my fingers and have 5,000 new young people in our movement by the end of this year. That's not going to happen. It's absolutely not going to happen because it's going to take time to plant those seeds, water them, and give them enough sun and space, and replant them in other places, for them to grow. It's gonna take a while before the work bears fruit. But we have to do that right now. I think traditionally our movement has not necessarily done that. It's so well connected, so well resourced. We should be taking a larger role in cultivating our young people. And I don't think that's what has happened because it wasn't a priority. And I'm not saying that it was a horrible thing, because prioritizing other things is what's given me the resources to be able to do these things. So, I'm not looking the gift horse in the mouth, or smirking the good work that was done ahead of me. But it's on my shoulders to figure it out. And so, yeah, there are some structural changes. Part of that is youth leadership development. I think it would be lovely for our boards to continually reserve space for young people. I've been on boards with young people, and they're good and kind people. They don't know how to work a board, but that's something we have to teach. We have to teach them how to steward organizations; we have to teach them what leadership looks like. They're so thoughtful and sharp, very sharp. These young folks are real, and they have their moments. But they're really, for the most part, really sharp. They're sharper than we give them credit for. And I don't think I have the wherewithal that they do at their age, in their late teens and early twenties. I don't think I was that smart. I don't think I connected all the dots and felt so strongly about things. They are sitting in such an uncomfortable position that many generations have not known. I think they have an awareness that the rest of us don't. But yes, there are some structural issues that need to change. For right now, my focus is going to be working on cultivating a really, really dynamic group of young folks. So, I'm working pretty closely with the Secular Student Alliance, working with humanist chaplains on campuses. I'm chatting with Greg Epstein, who's a humanist chaplain at Harvard and MIT. I'm talking with Anthony Cruz.[6] But yeah, it's building those bridges with young people. I didn't realize Secular Student Alliance even has chapters in like Middle School. I was like, oh, be still my heart. That's fantastic. And that's where we need to be. We need to be there together, and not in an extractive way. We don't need to be asking the kids to do anything, but how are we investing in them? How are we helping them with programming, with support? What kind of financial support are we offering? We need to draw stronger lines between Secular Student Alliance and American Humanist Association because when the kids leave high school and they go off to college, they're going to organize with Secular Student Alliance. But what if they're traveling and they get in trouble or something happens, or they just want to hang out with good people? They should be able to reach out to one of the American Humanist Association chapters. But they don't know that right now because we never cultivated that relationship. And we also need to address the absence of Black and brown people in leadership positions in this movement. For example, we can be intentional in our hiring; we can be intentional about the people that we bring to advise us as a movement. So that's one of the things that I'm thinking of—convening an Executive Advisory Council that works directly with me, that works directly with our directors. Because this is where change happens in our organization. There's another thing we need to be mindful of too: our culture. Who are we? Who do we want to be? What kind of work do we want to do as a movement? And how are we going to help our community do the work with us? I think we so idealistically want to do everything at one time, but you cannot do everything well. But again, partnerships are really important.

Anthony: It seems fairly obvious to me what humanists get wrong in terms of social justice, but what are humanists getting right?

Nadya: Honestly, there are a few things that humanists are getting right. As far as social justice goes, I think we all recognize how preserving first amendment rights, in keeping Church-State separation, benefits everyone. I think those are absolutely important justice issues. We shouldn't be in places and be put upon by the church. So, I think we've traditionally gotten that right. We've done that very well—lobbying around abortion rights, etc. Government shouldn't be in that at all. Voting Rights is another. I mean, thank Audre Lorde for Stacey Abrams and the crew in Georgia![7] What they did in Georgia was just beyond impressive. Those very broad issues that affect everyone really highlight how humanists believe in alleviating the human condition—equality, equal access. And there may be other places. I'm still learning, so there may be some other issue areas.

Anthony: I'm with you on this. I think you're on point. One last question for you. At one point you said every single issue in the social justice framework is a humanist issue. I agree with you, but I'm wondering that because we have limited resources, how do we prioritize around those issues?

Nadya: I think leaning in on climate justice, which is a threat multiplier, exacerbates every undergirding systemic oppression. We've got to get the climate under control. We've got to stop fossil fuel subsidies; we've got to stop pipelines because they're polluting our water, our air, our soil. I don't want to use the word "intersects," but literally it really does; it layers upon everything else. So, I think that's probably the first thing. The other is that we really, really need to talk about the "justice system." It's not justice. It's a holdover from slavery. When we're talking about the police, we're talking about the carceral system, we're talking about our prison system that treats people inhumanely and then expects them to come out and not reoffend. They are given no support; they get no real training. And then when they leave the prison, they're done with serving their sentence, but they can't get hired by those same companies they worked for while in prison as slave labor. It's absolutely insane that we expect something different to happen. But it's a human rights issue, and also a safety issue for those folks and for their families, for all of us. There's a hole in the justice system we need to look at. We need to have conversations about that. You and I both know housed within the justice system issue is racial justice and economic justice. They start criminalizing our Black boys and girls around the time they are fourth graders. They simply want a prison pipeline. They want prisoners; they don't want productive members of society; they don't want us, Black people, to be productive members of society. Black-on-Black crime is not the subject of the conversation. And if we're going to talk about it, we need to talk about white-on-white crime. People offend against people that they live around. So, white people rob white people. They buy drugs and sell drugs to white people. So, I'm saying that the carceral system in general—starting with the police and ending with prisons where people end up—and the support available when they come out is important. There are so many things, Tony. OMG! Another thing that we really need to address, that I think people don't think about, and which really bothers me, is Disability Justice. We're really ableist, a shitty ableist society. And it really is horrible. People don't think about disabled people who sit in the margins. There are disabled people in every demographic. There is intersectionality for them as there is for everyone else, but they're so invisible. They're made to be invisible, in every place that they sit, and we've got to do a better job. We humanists have to lead to ensure that our spaces are not ableist spaces, and the things that we say and do are not ableist. I have to work on this, and I think there are a lot of people in our movement who don't think about those things either.

Anthony: I lied. That wasn't the last question. You have my mind racing! So, I have to ask one more. What can the humanist movement learn from the Movement for Black Lives?[8] What should we be taking out of their playbook?

Nadya: Oh, man, so many things. Oh, stop gaslighting us and accept responsibility. Racism was not created by us. It was not created by Black and brown people. I don't think our indigenous brothers and sisters started any of that, you know. When the white folks came to Turtle Island, they were fed; they were clothed; and they were given fire to stay warm. We are hospitable people. Black and brown people are hospitable people. Because we didn't start racism, it is not for us to fix.

Black people, particularly in this country, tried to take advantage of opportunities during Reconstruction and thrived. We were everywhere, and we were doing the thing and they couldn't stand it. And that's when Jim Crow came around. Slavery is still here in our prison systems. Let's not discount that. So, when we are saying that Black Lives Matter (BLM), we mean please organize with us and call your white cousins out on their bullshit. It is not for us to do. We have got to save one another. We are literally in a constant state of panic. I can't speak for you, Tony. But I know I am, when I think about my father, my brothers, my cousins, my daughter, her father. I'm in a constant state of panic about us being stopped by the police, while walking, while shopping, while eating, while doing anything—even breathing while Black. And it is exhausting. We do not have the energy for it. We're trying to just get by. White people need to call out these violent, oppressive systems that *they* created, that are codified in our Constitution (the first iteration of it, not the amendments). This country isn't broken, no; it is working as they intended it to. Call it out! Do we need to write a new one? Maybe we do. Maybe we need a new constitution because the first one is broken. White folks need to organize themselves, and they need to call out their bullshit. We need to work on our own solutions for ourselves. We too recognize we've got to get our stuff together as a community; we do. We're not saying that we don't have problems, but we cannot fight you and fight this system at the same time either. We have to figure out our own solutions. We can take back our agency, but we can't do it if we're fighting you. So, yeah, BLM is really about calling white people to the carpet to fix their mess and respecting and acknowledging that we have been continually put upon daily in this country. The boot has continually been on the neck of Black Americans and has never let up. When are we gonna get some relief? When are we going to get reparations? It needs to happen. People need to get angry. White people, particularly those in our movement, need to get angry. They need to take the ball and run with it and go clean the situation up so that we can work on solutions, get ourselves together, and have a little rest.

What I want to convey most is that human kindness and care has to be the action that drives us forward as humanists, not just intellectual and academic pursuits. I have gone back to being totally disconnected from organized humanism, but still actively practice my core values of servant leadership, integrity, kindness, persistence, and community/togetherness. We lead as humanists by serving others with humility and abolishing harmful practices, not pontificating and condescending.

Anthony: You're speaking the truth. That's a mic-drop moment!

Nadya: I would, if I had a mic!

3

Freethought and Black Personhood

Christopher Cameron

Anthony: Today I have the pleasure of spending time talking with Dr. Christopher Cameron. Dr. Cameron holds a PhD in History from the University of North Carolina at Chapel Hill. And he's currently a professor of history at the University of North Carolina, Charlotte. He is also the founding president of the African American Intellectual History Society. And in addition to courses related to the intellectual history of the United States, he teaches one of the few courses in the United States dealing with unbelief. His publications include the *Abolitionist Movement Documents Decoded*, and the book we're going to chat about today, *Black Freethinkers: A History of African American Secularism*. Thanks for taking time to talk with me, Chris.[1]

Christopher: Thanks so much for having me.

Anthony: So let me start with this: You deal with the mechanisms for upliftment within African American communities, and you show the slow progress of change over time. What brought about this book? Why did you write it?

Christopher: There really was a confluence of different factors. One, in sort of mid- to late 2012, I was wrapping up revisions on my book, *To Plead Our Own Cause*, dealing with Puritanism and Black abolitionism in Massachusetts. Part of the process to finish the book was going through and filling in some citations and whatnot. And I came across Albert Raboteau's book *Slave Religion* in my footnotes, and something just prompted me to read the book.[2] Again, I hadn't read it since doing my comprehensive exams in graduate school. So, I went and just read it again, and I'm really, really glad I did because the first time around, I hadn't come across this line toward the very end of the book, where he says he'd gone through and explored the creation of a syncretic form of African American Protestantism. He says, of course, not all slaves believed in a just and benevolent God, who was looking out for their interests. Some simply couldn't reconcile their lives in slavery with the idea of a God. And so, I was like, huh, okay. He only has two paragraphs that provide a couple of examples of religiously skeptical slaves. That really piqued my interest. Right around the same time as this, I came across a YouTube video as part of a series called "Black Folk Don't," produced by Angela Tucker. One of the episodes of only five or six minutes was entitled "Black Folk Don't Do Atheism."[3] I was like, oh, really? I'd just read this little piece by Raboteau talking about atheistic slaves back in the 18th century. So that just prompted me to start looking. I had personally become an atheist, maybe two, two and a half years before that. Wrapping up my first book, I was looking for a new book project. I thought there could really be something here. So, I started looking for everything I could find. I started coming across blog posts from the organization African Americans for Humanism. I came across your book, *By These Hands*.[4] And I started to think that maybe there is something here and this could potentially be my next book project. So that's sort of how I got started on it in 2012. And seven years later, the book came out.

Anthony: Fantastic, fantastic. And I think you're absolutely right. You get historians and others who, in passing, will mention not all Black folks believed. But it's typically an aside even in light of Benjamin Mays' work, that wonderful book that chronicles critiques of the God ideas within Black religious thought and cultural production. Why do you think scholars have been so slow to investigate free thought within African American communities as a kind of robust alternate mode of thinking and doing?

Christopher: I think there are a couple of reasons for this. One has to do with the project of Black history in and of itself, which started largely as a political project aimed at combating racism—combating Jim Crow by showing positive examples of morally upright, respectable Black people who adhered to American values. They were patriots, they were good Christians, right? And this, I think, this mode of writing history, this kind of celebratory history, really dominated the field for many, many years. But, even more recently, I think if we're looking at scholarship over the past twenty or thirty years or so, that kind of respectability politics in the writing of Black history hasn't been quite as prevalent. Nevertheless, the overwhelming majority of African American historians themselves have been religious, and I think it's—Black nonbelief—just something that's not even really on their radar as a possibility, as something that's been significant within Black culture.

Anthony: So, Chris, as you think about the development of freethought in African American communities over the course of time, what are two or three of the values, two or three of the virtues, that really stand out?

Christopher: I would say the staunch importance of political engagement. One of the things that my book shows is right from the beginning, African American secularism was, in large part, intertwined with Black radical politics. And Black freethinkers never really had the sort of luxury of divorcing their secularism from their political commitments. So, for Black freethinkers—like Hubert Harrison, or Harry Heywood, or Louise Thompson Patterson, and others—their secular thought really informed how they thought about politics and how they engaged with politics.[5] Their secular thought pushed them toward more active political engagement. I think about people like James Forman, who in his book, *The Making of Black Revolutionaries*, talks about how he feels belief in God has hurt his people because it's caused them to look to heaven and develop an otherworldly outlook instead of taking action for themselves.[6] Now, this was something of an exaggeration, right, you have the Social Gospel?[7] True, for many people, religion didn't motivate political activism. But his was an exaggeration as some scholars have shown, especially regarding the period leading up to the 1930s–1940s. So, the importance of political engagement, I think, has really been central to Black free thought. And that's one thing that in many ways distinguishes it from the tradition of white secularism, which at times has been overly political; but, at other times that secularism has nothing to do with politics. It's an intellectual posture, against religion, and it can be divorced from the political realm. So, I think that's one and another is just sort of a questioning and kind of skeptical bent of mind, right? Not a mindset that doesn't allow for easy conformity to the norms of American society, and even the norms of African American society—just a questioning of everything that we know, and really trying to get at the truth using reason and human understanding.

Anthony: If free thought doesn't develop strictly as a rejection of the Black Church, can you highlight some of the other points of entry into free thought for Black folks?

Christopher: I think another main point of entry is a rejection of white supremacy. And that's probably even more important than a rejection of the Black Church. I found in the 1830s and 1840s that Black free thought grew out of lived experience of enslaved people who were looking at the hypocritical actions of their Christian masters, who would go to a church service on Sunday morning, and then physically assault or sexually assault their enslaved people on Sunday afternoon. So, I think one of the main origins of Black secularism in the United States is actually an engagement and struggle against slavery and white supremacy. And that even remains prominent in the twentieth century as well. That's the origins. And that's something that differentiates the beginnings of Black and white free thought, but that remained important throughout the twentieth century. We see these different kinds of inflection points where Black free thought becomes more popular at certain times. One of those inflection points is right about 1915–16 or so, which just so happens to coincide with renewed activity by the KKK, the creation of films like *Birth of a Nation* (which was played in Woodrow Wilson's White House), nativism and anti-communism with the Red Scare of 1919. This is one of the key waves of Black secularism, right? Susan Jacoby, in her book *FreeThinkers*, refers to the period from roughly 1875 to 1915 as the golden age of freethought. Well, the end of that period, I think, can be seen as a golden age of Black freethought, where you have some of the most prominent Black intellectuals, artists, and political figures becoming secularists.[8] And we see a similar dynamic in the civil rights era. This is another period when you start to see a lot more evidence of Black secularism. So, I think the struggle against white supremacy and racism, in addition to opposition to the Black Church and the cultural power of ministers, is another defining feature of Black freethought.

Anthony: In terms of Black humanists, atheists, and freethinkers, who participated historically in the struggle against injustice, what are some of the differences that their evolvement made in terms of the vision of justice? What sense of justice and which moral and ethical values guided their work?

Christopher: Sure, I think one of the key differences is the insertion of economic justice during the early 20th century. This is a period when you start to see a very close connection between critiques of capitalism, critiques of Christianity, and of imperialism, both at home and abroad. I'm thinking of figures like W. E. B Du Bois, Langston Hughes, Harry Haywood, and, perhaps most prominently, Hubert Harrison, who in a number of different writings linked together global white supremacy, capitalism, and Christianity. Harrison argued that discrimination against Black people was not only racist, but it was also classist. You start to see the beginnings of intersectionality in Black political life. And that would continue with some of the writings of people like Louise Thompson Patterson in some of her personal writings and Nella Larson's novel *Quicksand*, where you start to get gender considered.[9] This kind of intersection between race, class, and gender, which would prefigure the intersectionality that would come to dominate—not necessarily dominate, but be significant in Black intellectual life about fifty years later. We see some of these early Black freethinkers be pioneers in their critiques of patriarchy tied to their critiques of classism.

Anthony: Let's stick with Du Bois and let's add in James Weldon Johnson. We talked a little earlier about Christian influence—the use of Christian grammar and vocabulary. And it seems to me with these two figures, and there are others, you get freethinkers manipulating and altering this language, and seeing the cultural value in it while denying its theological importance. You get someone like James Weldon Johnson, who can appreciate the Black sermonic style—the way Black preachers do their thing.[10] He finds something compelling in their poetic expression, but sees the sermons as devoid of theological value. And with Du Bois, you get an appreciation for the Black Church; you get him providing prayers for Black people—using this prayer model as a poetic way of engaging a world that doesn't make a whole lot of sense.[11] But again, he is removing the theological trappings, the theological baggage typically associated with that language. Is this practice something prominent within Black freethought? Or are these two outliers?

Christopher: This is definitely prominent within Black freethought. You listed two of the key figures who take that approach, but we could also add Langston Hughes, Zora Neale Hurston, and probably most importantly James Baldwin[12] to that list. So, what they're doing is taking these key parts of African American religion, and using them for their own purposes. But it's also showing that African American culture more broadly has been influenced critically by these religious concepts and ways of being without necessarily having to believe in the God idea. One of the ways this came up is in multiple conversion to atheism narratives, where folks like Langston Hughes and James Forman were on the mourner's bench in their evangelical Black churches. They're describing a moment where they should have converted to Christianity. But instead, they faked such conversion. Writing from a distance, years down the line, they're actually telling us that these became the moments where they saw behind the veil, so to speak. And they actually became atheists at those moments. They were supposed to be Christian, right? Richard Wright has a similar experience in his autobiography, and there's this really interesting part where he's talking to some of his friends about their baptism.[13] And his friends admit to him that they don't believe in the power of baptism; they don't believe that anything happened. They just go along with the process. So, these practices—being baptized, being up on the mourner's bench, adopting a particular rhetorical style, even using highly religious language—don't necessarily have to mean belief in God. Instead, these things have simply become broader elements of Black culture, right?

Anthony: That's an interesting point. We can occupy more than one social space simultaneously. We are complex that way, and that brings me to a point you raised concerning another extremely prominent figure. You say at one point in your book that Frederick Douglass expressed deistic and agnostic views at times; and, he was a religious liberal and humanist. Can you help me think through how Frederick Douglass held in creative tension those various points of view?

Christopher: Douglass, to me, is really one of the more interesting figures in the history of Black religion, and he is one person who's been all over the religious spectrum. The in-depth biography of him, by David Blight, argues that his religious faith formed a sort of prophetic style that guided his life and activism, and many other scholars have argued for the importance of Christian identity or religion in his life. I don't necessarily disagree.[14] But I do argue that we have to look at the entirety of his life, not just select moments, and we must seriously engage with his statements that were critical of or dismissive of religion. They don't do that. Some scholars ignore his statements that are dismissive of religion. When we do look at those, I think he should be seen as a freethinker. At certain moments in his life, he questioned whether God existed, or whether we could know God existed. At other moments, he actively stated that God did not exist. But at other times, Douglass referenced believing in God, while at the same time doubting God's sovereignty and omnipotence. This comes out most clearly in the final meeting of the American antislavery society in 1870, which I believe you discuss in your book titled *By These Hands*. He's at this last meeting of some of the most prominent abolitionist and activists in the country. People are thanking God for freeing the slaves. Douglass rose and said, I like to thank men; I like to thank the men and women who ran away and voted for freedom with their feet. And he says, it's only through the actions of such individuals that I can come to know God at all. For me, another interesting aspect of Douglass are views that place him within the bounds of American religious liberalism, whereby he could also be seen as a transcendentalist. (This is what I'm working on now—a history of Black Unitarians and Universalists.[15]) The idea of transcendentalism, most simply, is a belief in the divinity of the human—a reverence for nature, a notion that human values and morality come from our own reasoning and experience. We create our own values in the here and now, so you don't necessarily need to rely on sacred texts and sacred books.

Anthony: If you think across humanist organizations, for example, it seems to me the wrong question often dominates. That wrong question is the question of why Black people embrace a religion that was used to enslave them. It seems to me there's a better question to ask: Why hasn't humanism been more appealing?

Christopher: Exactly. Yeah, I was just talking to somebody about this at the Freedom from Religion Foundation conference a couple of weeks ago. I get this question often. And it's often phrased as: Why are Black people so religious? And, I respond, why aren't white freethinkers doing a better job of bringing Blacks and Latinos and other races into the fold? So, I think we can flip that around. To me that question is based off of racist assumptions about the barbarism and savagery of African Americans that goes back, of course, to the beginning of the slave trade, but we can even see it very prominently in the writings and speeches of nineteenth-century white freethinkers. Nathan Alexander, has just published a really great book called *Race in a Godless World*, where he explores the intersections of race and atheism in the United States and Britain from about the Civil War till the start of the First World War.[16] And one of the things that he shows is that there were a lot of white freethinkers in the late 19th century, who bought lock, stock, and barrel into the common racist assumptions of their day and argued that basically African Americans were too savage, too barbarous, and lacked the capabilities for critical thought and reason, and, thus, could not be a part of the freethought fold. It was a convenient excuse to segregate African Americans from the broader freethought movement. I think we see lingering effects of that notion, even if we don't have the outright or hostile racist statements that we saw back then. There's still this notion that Black people are more emotional than reasonable or logical. And that's one of the things that keeps them tied to the Black Church instead of embracing secularism.

Anthony: I think that's absolutely correct. And I think humanist organizations often work based upon a false premise—that if you free yourself from religion, you free yourself from harmful ideologies. As a result, these organizations don't adequately address white privilege. Right? For example, separation of church and state is extremely important and science education is extremely important, but neither one of those would have kept Trayvon Martin alive, or George Floyd alive, or Breonna Taylor alive. Right? Addressing anti-Black racism requires tackling white supremacy and white privilege as part of our agenda within humanist organizations. The humanist movement writ large, it seems to me, has been too weak when it comes to this kind of internal critique of the white privilege and white supremacy that live within these movements.

Christopher: Absolutely, I think Sikivu Hutchinson probably explores this better than anyone in her books, *Mortal Combat: Black Atheists, Gender Politics, and the Value Wars* and *Godless Americana*.[17] In those books, she's looking at the history and contemporary politics of secular and humanist organizations, and showing that if humanist organizations want to appeal to Black people, one of the things they need to do is take on some of the functions that Black churches have taken on and failed to do adequately. So, they need to start actively working to address things like the school-to-prison pipeline, or housing disparities, or lack of affordable housing, health care disparities. If folks don't have enough food to eat, they're not going to hear your message of secularism, right? It's not just that people aren't looking toward reasonable ideas. They're looking toward ideas that also mesh with their lived reality. If Black folks start seeing white humanists out here, protesting alongside them, and building institutions alongside them, and contributing to a more just world, that is going to make humanism more appealing to Black people.

Anthony: In some circles, it seems to me, there's an implicit assumption that critique is activism. Right? I'm critiquing the Black Church, so I'm all about the well-being of Black people—as opposed to recognizing that the advancement of Black people, the ending of anti-Black racism, requires something of white people well beyond critique. They have to give something up.

Christopher: Yeah, and it's kind of funny because even though I'm an atheist, and I critique the Black Church, I don't really like it when white people do it! I'm like, you know, I don't necessarily get down with the Black Church but it's still *our* church. Just that critique and the lack of substantive action rings really hollow. And that at times rings a little racist, right? You're just critiquing our church, but not offering or supporting any alternatives. So yeah, I totally agree with you there.

Anthony: I think that's absolutely right. And I often say to my friends who are deep into the Black Church that there is something that the Black Church can do—it can surrender its privilege. If you are really about the well-being of folks within the communities in which you operate, pay property taxes! Yep. Put that money into the local economy. That will make a difference in that folks will then be able to establish themselves because they will have economic resource allowing them to revitalize their communities. They need to be able to purchase stuff; they don't need prayer. And so, this is a real way in which churches can say we are about the business of transforming society. We are going to reject this privilege, and we are going to pay our property taxes!

Christopher: Yep, pay property taxes, and also don't rely on the labor of volunteers, right? This promise that if you work for the kingdom of God, you'll be compensated later on. Pay taxes and also hire local people in the community! You have these million-dollar churches in really blighted and depressed areas with high unemployment rates, health care disparities, and struggling schools. Not just their tax dollars, but also their ability to hire people in that community would really help them.

Anthony: That is absolutely right! Read James Forman's critique.[18] Read that message he delivered at Riverside Church because it gives some sense of the economic obligations and opportunities available to religious organizations. It also strikes me that one of the things that we have to unlearn from Black churches is how to think about expertise. Black churches are one of the few businesses in which a willing heart is sufficient to hold positions, that a willing heart becomes the only necessary criterion for holding high-level positions. We have to really begin to rethink how we value expertise, how we value skill sets.

Christopher: Yeah, I absolutely agree. That brings to mind an experience I had here in Charlotte, where my wife and I went to this evangelical Black Church. And one of the main messages that we got from the minister was to put aside our reason and just trust in the Lord. And I'm like, if we put aside our reason, it's going to be pretty hard to solve some of the problems that we have, not only in the city of Charlotte, but in our state and in our nation at large. I think too often that one of the messages we get is that reason, higher learning, is not as important as just being right with God and having a good heart. Accepting Jesus as your Lord and Savior.

Anthony: That's interesting. That kind of anti-intellectualism is a part of the Black Church's legacy. And I'd say on the flip side, within secular organizations, there can often be a kind of anti-cultural stance. That is to say, for example, a deep suspicion and denial of ritual, of meaning-making processes. And this rejection of the more affective dimensions of human need prevents us from providing a soft place for folks to land. These humanist organizations are not anti-intellectual. They're all about reading books, but they're opposed to the cultural mechanisms that folks have used to make life meaningful.

Christopher: Yeah, yeah, absolutely. I just started reading Sasha Sagan's book, *For Small Creatures Such as We*, which explores the importance of ritual for human beings in general.[19] And this speaks to a sort of broader cultural influence of African American religion beyond theism in that another function that churches often serve beyond the social and the educational is marking the really important and significant moments in people's lives, and providing structure and order. And there's a place for that, right? You don't necessarily have to believe in God to believe that it's important to have some sort of ceremony to mark an important moment or an important event in your life.

And this is why we see folks like Mandisa Thomas, founder of the organization Black Nonbelievers,[20] being an official humanist celebrant so that she can provide some of these rituals for people.

Anthony: So, Chris, as you go from location to location, talking about your book, what would you say is the biggest misconception concerning Black freethought held by folks?

Christopher: I would say probably the biggest misconception is that free thought, in general, emerged out of the European enlightenment, and that it is something alien to Black culture. One of the critiques of secularism I've heard, when I present at academic conferences and other venues, is that it's solely a Western construction or ideology that doesn't have any relevance to Black life. But an indigenous form of secularism emerged in the United States that grew out of the lived experiences of enslaved people. So, they didn't have to read Voltaire to know that something was off about the idea of a God who loved them and cared for them.[21] These are organic intellectuals who observed what was happening around them and concluded that there was no God. That's one misconception about freethought, in general, but for Black freethought, it's probably just the misconception that it doesn't exist. I know you've been working in this field for probably twenty-five years. But most of the books on this topic are still your own, I would say 90 percent of them. Right? When I began my work, what surprised me the most was how few historians had actually taken up this topic. Especially since, you published *By These Hands* in 2003, which—if you follow the threads of the primary sources—takes you through the history of Black secularism dating back to the nineteenth century. One more misconception about Black freethought is that it never became as extensive as white freethought due to the innate religiosity of African Americans. And this again, speaks to what we were just discussing—that this is some sort of intellectual failure on the part of Black people, rather than just a simple failure of white freethinkers to appeal to a Black audience.

Anthony: You mentioned *By These Hands*, so I have to give a shout-out to Norm Allen because that book builds on his earlier work.[22] Chris, you've been generous with your time, so I'm going to limit myself to one last question. As you were doing the research for this project, and as you were writing the book, what's the thing that shocked you most? What is the thing that you discovered that just kind of threw you?

Christopher: What shocked me most was really how significant this history of Black secularism has been—and the fact that in every major intellectual political movement in African American history dating back to the struggle against slavery, it's prominent and, in some cases, leading these movements. If you read chapter two of my book, for example, it pushes us to think about the Harlem Renaissance as a secular culture, a movement dominated by freethinkers, not just a few but dominated from the start by figures like James Weldon Johnson, Du Bois, Langston Hughes, Nella Larsen, and Claude McKay.[23] And I could go on, but throughout the entirety of African American history, Black freethinkers might not have been numerically dominant, but they were so critical in our key intellectual, political, and cultural movements. So that was probably the most shocking thing because I had read a lot of African American and American History prior to starting this book and it's just something that had not come up.

4

Seeing the Secular

Phil Zuckerman

Anthony: Today I get to talk with my colleague and friend, Dr. Phil Zuckerman. He is a professor of sociology and secular studies at Pitzer College in Claremont, California, and he's also affiliated faculty with Claremont Graduate University. Anyone who is unfamiliar with his tremendous scholarship—well, it's time to catch up! He's the author of numerous books, including *The Oxford Companion to Secularism*, and *Society Without God*.[1] Phil, we go back a good number of years. I think our first encounter revolved around the book you were working on dealing with W. E. B. Du Bois.[2] For both of us, that was fairly early in our careers. I'm gonna put it this way: I met you during my pre-baldness years. And we've worked together a good number of years in the post-baldness era.

Phil: Well said, well said. Thanks, Tony.

Anthony: I'm just keeping it real.

Phil: That's right. That's right. It's so true. Well, thanks for that introduction. And you know, you're just such a bright shining star out there in the cosmos. So, I'm just happy and honored to be with you. You've been so kind and gracious to me over the years, in many ways. It's always a pleasure.

Anthony: We've had some opportunities to chat a bit, but I've never had an opportunity to really dig deep. Right? So, I'd like to start this way: Folks come into the Academy for a variety of reasons, but what led you to the Academy. Why do you do what you do?

Phil: Well, I was trying to find a cure for my baldness, to be honest. I thought you might have some tips. Yeah, that's an interesting question. I grew up in LA, near Santa Monica, and the film business was everywhere. Everybody was in the film business. I actually was into theater, acting, and drama. I was always involved in school plays and school musicals. I loved to perform. But I also liked to debate and discuss, and I was always very interested in current events. I read the news constantly. So, it was this weird mix, because I, on the one hand, hung out with thespians, who were not always interested in politics. Or, I always had a book with me, even when I was a young man. I first went to junior college out of high school. Because I was trying to pursue acting, I stayed in LA. And my folks said, well, if you want to live at home, you have to still be in school full time, or you have to get out and support yourself. So I went to junior college, great school, Santa Monica City College, and was pursuing acting. But I remember, it struck me, I used to go to the casting calls, and I'd be the only guy with a book in the casting room. And this is before iPhones, nobody had iPhones. We'd all be sitting in the casting lounges, and they thought I was weird for reading. I always had that interest. After a couple of years of realizing there was no way I was going to be able to support myself through acting. I would get jobs, but the money wasn't consistent. So even if you got a gig, how long was that check? So, I finally transferred to the University of Oregon. And it was like I was home. I felt so good! And I felt so comfortable, and I just excelled. I actually didn't do well in high school. I struggled a lot. I'm not a good test-taker. Math is very challenging for me. I always did well in English and maybe social studies. I struggled in the sciences and math. At Santa Monica City College, I took sociology for the first time. And that was a game changer! I got straight As in that. When I got to the University of Oregon, I just loved academia. I loved that I could sit, learn, discuss, and talk about the world. And I never left. I'm a full professor, and I'm an associate dean. But still, when I get paid each month, I'm just like, seriously, I get paid to do this?! I'm reading books; I'm writing shit; I'm having discussions with my students. So, to me, it's just a dream.

Anthony: See, now you're telling our secrets!

Phil: It's so funny. Because sometimes I'm on Twitter, and I'm linked to a lot of academics on Twitter. And a lot of people in the academic world just complain and complain and complain. They talk about how awful it is and how bad the pay is. And how bad the hours are. And I'm always scratching my head, like, are you serious? I don't deny *their* experiences. I think their reality is true. But for me, getting paid to teach, read, and write has never felt bad. I mean, I run to work every day. I run to work. I run to my office because I'm so happy here. So, I guess I just lucked out.

Anthony: Why sociology? I majored in sociology as an undergrad. And, for me, urban sociology was a welcome invitation to explore the world—to explore the sort of neighborhoods that produced me. And I could go into these neighborhoods, and the fallback position wasn't, "Oh, how could you be from there?" A real curiosity was encouraged. And so, I found that really thrilling, but what brought you to sociology?

Phil: Yeah, I didn't even know what sociology was in high school. It wasn't discussed. I learned history, economics. I didn't even know what it was. I remember my dad saying, "you might want to take a sociology class." I always say to my students, when they asked me, "what's the difference between sociology and psychology?" I say, well, people who have problems with society major in sociology. People who have problems with themselves major in psychology. There's some truth to it in that all four of my grandparents were refugees from Europe—hunted Jews. From that I was sensitive to inequality, persecution, injustice. And I was always curious about inequality, racism, sexism, homophobia. These things bothered me. And it's interesting because, even though I grew up in a very privileged neighborhood, I just happened to be going into fourth grade when the LA Unified School District decided to initiate mandatory busing. In other words, there was a recognition that the LA City Unified School District, which I believe was the largest in the country at the time, was grossly divided by race and class, which were totally intersecting. You had some schools that were just underfunded and underperforming; and you had these other great schools. And somebody said, this isn't okay; we're all one school district. We're gonna bus people all over. We're gonna bus people from this part of town to here, and this part of town over there. And 80 percent of the kids in my neighborhood just pulled out of the public school system. A startup private school popped up in the neighborhood, and they all went to that little village school. My parents said, "no, you go to public school." I was bused to Baldwin Hills. I was bused to Coliseum Street elementary school for three years. And it was profound. I mean, it was fantastic. You couldn't not think about race and class. Primarily those I would say. I wasn't too attuned to other issues, although I remember when all the Iranians showed up in 1979, fleeing the revolution in Iran. So, I don't know when I got to sociology—sorry, this is a longwinded answer—here was a class that was specifically addressing race, class, gender. I remember those were the big three. And we talked about social problems, such as inequality. I remember reading *Crisis in American Institutions*.[3] I also was blown away by C. Wright Mills—these basic insights on how we are shaped by these forces.[4] Whether we recognize them or not, they are shaping our lives and our identities. It made sense to me, and I ran with it. I loved learning about social movements and social change. I liked the way sociologists seemed to care about the world. And I'll end here: I remember when I was in graduate school, at the University of Oregon, which was a big university, we organized the graduate student union—got excellent health insurance. Eighty percent of the organizers of that union were sociology grad students! There's something to be said for that. But now as I'm older, I'm actually reading a lot more philosophy, a ton of history. Even evolutionary psychology, believe it or not, has helped me understand some things. But I've always felt at home among sociologists.

Anthony: I've always been of the opinion that if we do this education thing right, it changes us. We can't be on a campus for four years, be vulnerable to what that experience can entail, and leave the same way we arrived. So, how did your time in higher education as a student change you?

Phil: Wow, man, it's hard because it's also such a significant age in and of itself; it is such a transformative age. I moved away from home. But specifically, if I think about the education, hopefully it made me less provincial. I think it made me open up. What it did for me was two things. One, it confirmed things I always felt or thought about the world. I've always thought that and here's John Stuart Mill saying it, or here's somebody from a different country saying it from a different part of the group.[5] And there's something very profound about that. It makes you feel more alive; it makes you feel more grounded. And it also makes you feel a little bit more connected to the stars or something. I'm thinking about the stars a lot today. So that was important. But also, it expanded my understanding of things. I'm thinking anecdotes, I hope that's okay. I'll give you a perfect example. I was taking French, which was a huge mistake, sorry French speakers. But if you live in southern California, taking French is about as useful as learning how to hunt elk, or something. I should have taken Spanish. But anyway, I was taking French and I remember showing up to a French conversation class. And there was another student there, a student activist. And I walked up and I said, did you see that girl out there on the quad handing out those flyers about stopping the war? I knew this person would be interested. We were both in the student activist realm. And she said, really, there was a girl out there handing out flyers? She said, was she in, like, fourth grade? And I said, huh? And she said, well, you said there was a girl standing in the quad. So, I'm just wondering how old was she? And why wasn't she in school? And I remember thinking, like, oh, come on, you know what I mean? And she was just, like, well, I'm just trying to get a sense of what you're talking about. Did you mean a girl? Or was it a woman? How old was she? And I was, like, eighteen, nineteen, twenty. It was a huge paradigm shift for me. She was right! Why would I call her a girl? I wouldn't have said, boy—maybe guy or dude; but I wouldn't have said, boy. And there were so many moments like that, and they helped me see the world differently. They helped put me in my place. They helped me stay humble. So, to me, education was about being less provincial in the world, and also just becoming more aware of other people's experiences and perspectives.

Anthony: All of these experiences we have on these campuses, all that we're learning in classrooms that affirms or challenges us, we filter through something, right? Some folks will filter that information through their church experience, or their synagogue experience, or their mosque experience. What did you filter your education through?

Phil: Even though I was raised very culturally Jewish—again, four refugees, all Jewish from Europe. My father's first language was Yiddish. He was a Yiddish teacher. Even though I was very ethnically Jewish, much more than most American Jews, we were all secular on the belief spectrum. My grandparents were nonbelievers. Two grandparents on my father's side were poor, uneducated, never went past grade school, didn't have running water—and they were hardcore atheists of the socialist stripe. They felt that religion was part of the problem; they were anti-religious. My mom's parents were a bit more upper-middle-class bohemian from Bohemia, German-speaking, and highly assimilated. And they just were more interested in literature, music, and films, more so than religion. So, they weren't anti-religious; they just had other things on their plate—more agnostic benignly so. I'm a third-generation nonbeliever. Even though we did ethnic Jewish things—like celebrate certain holidays, eat certain foods, and primarily hang out with other ethnic Jews as our social circle—there was no belief. I was never told there was a God; I was never told there was a heaven or hell; I was never told that prayer works. I was never told that angels or demons were out there. None of that was part of my world. So, I did filter my experiences in education through a very secular, humanist framework—the secular meaning no supernatural beliefs, and the humanist part, as you talk in your work, being those more positive values. But I remember again, and here's an anecdote from my time at the University of Oregon, there used to be preachers in the main quad in front of the Herb Memorial Union. And I was dumbfounded and riveted. What, I thought this happened in the 1600s! I would channel my inner actor. I would sometimes wrap a sweatshirt around my head, and I would go down there and pretend to be a little devil, and I would mock them. I had, like, 150 people laughing their asses off. Every time they'd say something, when there was a pause, I'd say, how hot is hell?! Tell us how hot hell is! And this used to kill the crowd. So, I didn't see religion and just shrug my shoulders and walk on. I felt like I had to engage it, and had to debunk it, for better or for worse. I wrote the atheist column in the student radical paper on campus. I guess I was always filtering stuff through that framework of secular humanism, for sure.

Anthony: You were doing the damn thing! You know, Phil, it sounds like, as an undergraduate, you reached a point where you thought this intellectual world is for me. I'm an academic! And I'm wondering, when you reached a point where secular humanism wasn't simply your family stance, but you actively claimed it. What was the point at which you claimed it personally, that you said, I'm a secular humanist?

Phil: Wow, man, that's a good question. It was early, pretty early on. I remember being in junior high and having arguments. I remember being profoundly confused that seemingly thoughtful, nice, normal people could believe what to me seemed manifestly insane. And I know that there's no way to say that nicely. But I'm just speaking from the gut here. I remember my first serious girlfriend, I was in tenth grade, and she was in eleventh grade. And we were in the same classes at school. We had the same social circles. I was madly in love with her. And her father was an evangelical, nondenominational preacher from Kansas or Oklahoma, I can't remember which. But he'd come out to Santa Monica to save the heathen. I was at her house all the time. Her parents were so nice. Her dad actually was not my stereotypical version of a preacher. He was a calm, bookish man with little glasses; and there was nothing about him that screamed fire and brimstone. They finally invited me to church one day, and I don't know if I'd ever been to church. It was this huge warehouse that they had converted into a church. And I was just dumbfounded. I couldn't believe what I was seeing and hearing and that might make me sound like an asshole or something. I understood the power of the community, but what is happening? I remember, for example, very clearly, at one point in the service, they call up this young couple, crying and holding a newborn baby. And I remember my girlfriend's dad saying, well, this is so and so and so and so. Their baby was born sixteen days ago with a terrible heart defect. Let's all pray and beg God to cure this baby's heart. I'm thinking here's a couple in their early twenties. Their first child, who's alive now, is about to die because it was born with a defective heart. And my girlfriend's dad is asking everybody to pray for this baby. I remember that my heart went out to this couple. I was devastated. And I thought how wonderful that they're surrounded by so much love, so much care, but what is happening? These people think that through the magic of mental emails, a magical invisible being will cure this baby. What is this saying, if they didn't pray, God wouldn't save the baby? The whole thing was just crazy to me. I remember thinking this is really sad. We went home that night, and I remember talking to my girlfriend, asking her if she really believed that stuff. She talked me through all her beliefs, from the rapture to Armageddon. I remember feeling scared; it freaked me out. And I think, to be quite honest, there is a part of me that's scared by certain forms of religion. I am totally comfortable in a sort of liberal, progressive religious environment.

I went to Episcopalian summer camp for years, and I even worked there. But that kind of fundamentalist faith—whether it's Jewish, Christian, Muslim, Hindu, whatever—scares me. I think it's a force for ill in the world, even though I understand that people in desperate circumstances need that comfort. It's not my place to take that away from them. I don't have anything better to offer. So, I've always had a kind of skeptical view. I didn't call it secular humanism, because I didn't know those words. But I do remember being in college, walking into the college library, and seeing the *American Atheist Magazine* in the racks.[6] I flipped out. I immediately subscribed. I think I wrote them a letter, and I was invited to speak at one of their meetings. I couldn't go to wherever the meeting was, but I was excited to know it existed. I'll end with this: I was also very involved in the Jewish student union. And to me, again, it was about community. It was an ethnic Association, and I was always planning activities, events, and bringing speakers. But I was living with other students in Oregon who weren't Jewish, who didn't know much about Jews. I remember one day someone said to me that they didn't know anybody as religious as me. That person couldn't have said anything worse. It was as if I was this active Catholic or this active Mormon, you know? I told him I'm an atheist. But his response was that I was always doing Jewish stuff. I tried to explain that Jews are kind of different—a people with a religion. It was hard to explain. When I got out of college and went into grad school, I drifted away from finding community among fellow Jews, and finding it more among humanists. I started learning about humanist organizations, and I started learning about secular humanism. It progressed from there.

Anthony: Let's shift gears a little bit, Phil. You get your first job. You're an academic, and you're getting a paycheck for it. Were you vocal about your disbelief as a faculty member? Did people know?

Phil: Yes, I can't help it! I had no filter. I have no filter at faculty meetings. I mean, it is ugly. And it wins me some friends, and it brings me some enemies. But, yes, I was very upfront. I started teaching "Introduction to Sociology," "Classical Social Theory," and "Sociology of Deviance." I was teaching "Sociology of Religion." I was very explicit. I would say to them, look, I'm a nonbeliever. In fact, much of my fascination with this work is trying to understand why people are religious? What is the good and bad that religion does in society? I'd tell them that they are gonna get an unfiltered secular take. However, I invite different religious speakers to this class—the Imam, Rabbi, a priest, a pastor, a minister. And that's how I countered the secular take. But yes, I've always been pretty vocal. Now at Pitzer College, which is a very secular school, it is no big deal. In fact, I rarely get believers. But I remember one time when I first was at Pitzer, I was giving a lecture on Mormonism, how it started, and I said, here's a great example of a religion that started recently. We have all the information you could ever dream of—its founders, how it grew, and how it developed. I gave a lecture on the frauds, scams, and cons of Joseph Smith. I talked about how he faked writing the *Book of Mormon* and how his friend, Martin Harris, helped him. I talked about his desire to sleep with young women.[7] I kind of went through everything to explain the origins of Mormonism. Well, that afternoon, one of the better students in class knocked on my door and said, look, I've been enjoying your class. It's amazing. But I'm Mormon. I've never heard the things you've said. Within five minutes, she was crying, right? Just crying about the most offensive thing she'd ever heard. This was an attack on her God, on her prophet, on her family, on her grandparents who suffered. I'm sitting there going, like, I just laid out the facts. Do you want to see my sources? I presented them in the lecture, but you can see them here. I didn't say that, but that's what I was thinking in my mind. I said I'm really sorry. I tried to be kind. But she ended up dropping the class and leaving Pitzer because it just was not the place for her. But I know that if I'd gotten hired in other parts of the country, I probably would have had a much rougher road because I'm very explicit. I remember about five or six years into teaching the "Sociology of Religion" class, a student said to me, I took this class because I wanted to learn about religion. And you do a lot of debunking of religion, which is fine; but that's not really the class I thought I was taking. And I said, you're right, and I retooled it to be more about looking at religion in society—how religion intersects with race, class, gender, politics, media, without the debunking. I've just started teaching a new class called "Secularism and Skepticism," or something like that, and with that class it's just truth in advertising. So, in that class, I could debunk religion and that will be that. And in the other class there's less debunking. That was really the birth of secular studies for me, because when I started teaching that class on secularism, skepticism, and religion, it was hugely popular. I had many students say to me, this is what I wanted. I'm majoring in religious studies, but this is actually what I wanted. I didn't want to read about church history. I didn't want to read about biblical interpretations. In a sense, I am glad that students said what they said to me, because it helped me make things clearer in my teaching.

Anthony: I want to get to secular studies, but your reflections sparked a few thoughts for me. I'd like to toy with those for a bit. It seems to me that within humanist community the typical strategy is to hit theists often and hard. But it strikes me that within the context of our professional work, our responsibility is to instill in students an appreciation for critical thinking and effective communication strategies. We are rocking students' worlds. So, I'm curious, particularly in light of the example you gave, what your strategy is for this sort of interrogation. Students come with eighteen years of unchallenged thinking on topics, and what is your strategy for tackling those areas, getting students to think critically concerning what they have always assumed? I believe we have a moral and ethical obligation to lead students through this process of interrogation and reconstitution. And so, again, what's your process for this work? And in terms of that process or strategy, what elements do you think ought to be employed within the larger humanist community?

Phil: Wow. Okay, those are big questions and important questions—moral and ethical imperatives in a sense. I'm hearing two things. One is how do I get my students to think critically, what are my strategies for that. And then the next one is shifting those strategies to the humanist world specifically, right?

Anthony: And with the students, how do you help them deal with the trauma that is a natural part of that interrogation, that critical engagement?

Phil: I would say sometimes I do it better. Sometimes I do it worse.

Anthony: Don't we all?

Phil: Yeah, for me that journey really takes place when I teach "Introduction to Sociology." And that's why I still love teaching it after all these years. I start with some key things like the social construction of reality. And we break that down. And I try to get them to ask questions, like how many aspects of our world feel normal? Feel natural? Feel permanent? And yet only exists because people say they exist and act accordingly? We talk about everything from beauty standards to what is a family? What is a race? What are countries? I can see, for some students, there's a real shift; they're suddenly like, wait a minute. We bring it to ourselves and we say, well, what about us is inborn and innate? What about us is only what it is or the way it is because of how we were raised, where we were raised, and the things we experienced? We even make lists. Sometimes I say, okay, make a list of three things about yourself that are uniquely you. These can be "I am" statements, I "like" statements, "I believe" statements. I say, don't worry, no one's gonna see this, so you can write whatever you want: I love apples. I love Led Zeppelin—whatever it is.[8] Then I say, okay, look at your statements, and then we start asking questions, and I say how many of the three would be the same if you had grown up in Yemen? Then we just kind of keep doing that. How many of these would be the same if you were a different gender? For some students, the exercise freaks them out. Am I only in college because my parents expected this of me? Am I only pro-abortion because of who raised me? We talk about race, and I ask about their beliefs concerning race—and would their beliefs be the same if they were white and lived in Alabama during the days of slavery? In 1851, would you have these same views? So, that's where I provide most of my critical thinking and classical theological theory—reading Marx, reading Du Bois, reading Durkheim.[9] And this work is broad enough so that they don't feel like they're specifically being attacked. I'm not specifically saying your views are socially constructed, or your identity is problematic, or you benefit from certain privileges. It's very broad so they can start to make those connections themselves. And some make those connections to the extreme, some not at all. But I really find that an enjoyable journey for myself as well. When it gets to the humanist world, I struggle with this, Tony. I just am really struggling. Forgive me if I'm ranting, but I'm looking at the world right now, and I'm looking at an attorney general in Texas who wants to imprison consenting adults who have non-procreative sex. He wants to criminally charge them. We have a Supreme Court justice who wants to revisit these rulings that abolished sodomy laws in our nation. We have a good chunk of the Unites States who believe Trump actually won the 2020 election. I could go on—women's bodily autonomy, gay rights, the environment. I'm just looking at this, and I know it's not true, but I keep blaming religion. I know that it's stupid; I know that it is sloppy thinking because most religion is a force for good. Most religious people are doing good things and have good hearts. And I know religious people that I'm thinking are a specific Christian nationalist, conservative strain. I know that and, yet, I'm having a hard time not seeing a certain version of a Jesus-centered, God-centered faith spearheading all this. When I read about the text messages between Ginny Thomas and Mark Meadows on January 6—that this was all for the glory of the King of Kings—it fucking freaked me out. I know fully well that many of those progressive, democratic congress people who were cowering in the Capitol that day are God believers, and Jesus believers. I know in my mind these things exist in the same way. But I think many people, when they look at a freaky world, or a scary world, need something to blame. And for some people, it's capitalism. For some people, it's racism. For some people, it's nationalism. To make sense of the world, we go into sloppy, simplistic thinking. I know if I really step back as a sociologist, I actually do believe that this Christian nationalism is actually rooted in racism, is actually rooted in nationalism, and is actually rooted in all these deeper sociological things. But for some reason, those are harder for me to grasp. They're harder for me to fight. If I can just blame religion, I can focus; I can channel. I know that's not the right way to do it. I know that we need allies, whatever our beliefs are. We need to embrace people of faith who share our politics. I remember, this is when my secular humanist activism was really challenged; it was the Georgia Senate election. And I think it was between a Trumper and Raphael Warnock. The balance of the Senate was gonna hang on this election. And this guy, Warnock, is a pastor, a Bible-quoting pastor, and I'm sending money to him! So, clearly my problem wasn't with religion. Because why would I support this candidate who's a strong Christian. I supported him because we have the same politics and he's going to save the world in a way that I want the world to be saved. Things are complex, so I struggle in humanist circles to get secular humanists to step back and realize we can't blame religion for all of society's problems. If religion vanished tomorrow, not all society's problems would vanish with it. Sikivu Hutchinson taught me that. I do believe certain forms of religion contribute to those problems, making them worse. But it's more complex so I would want my secular humanist brothers and sisters to not do what I often do—which is to assume religion is the problem. No, it's actually the case that certain forms of religion are problematic in certain ways. And that's my battle, but not the only battle.

Anthony: That's nuanced, and I like it. I would make a distinction between religion and theism. It seems to me that for secular humanists the real target is theism. It is often the case that this attack on theism really involves a "the best defense is a good offense" strategy. That is to say, the critique of theism frees secular humanists from having to look at their own shit. Right? If we blame religion for everything, we don't have to look at the ways in which we're sexist, or transphobic, or racist because it's really these religious people who cause these social problems. So, I like that nuance you offer. I think you do a fabulous job of describing the world. The world that we have produced is fucked, and this is not the consequence of divine anger or divine correction. We human beings have fucked up the social world and the earth. And every year we send students into this world, and here's my question: What are the values you hope to instill in students as they move from the safety of your campus into the world? What kind of values do you want them to take with them? That is to say, what kind of tools do you want to equip the students with as they move into and try to change the world?

Phil: Wow, okay, Tony, I got a laundry list here. First of all, I want to affirm what you just said. It's so true about the difference between theism and religion, and all that stuff. And I have thoughts on that. But let me get to my laundry list. Number one, a certain understanding of empiricism—that there is some kind of perceptible reality that responds to our senses. This allows us to build bridges that don't collapse; it allows you and I to have this conversation right now, even though you're 1000s of miles away. We now live in a world where truth is under assault—and I don't mean subjective, aesthetic truths—I mean reality, like how many people voted for a certain candidate, okay? So, I want my students to have an understanding and appreciation for certain empirical claims. Now, not all claims are empirical. I'm not saying everything can be reduced to empiricism. But empirical claims that are made should be able to be tested. And there's ways to test those claims. For me, right now, whether we're talking climate change, whether we're talking presidential elections, whether we're talking what contributes to gun violence, we need to be empirical on those matters. Next, I think students are hungry for a sense of how we can disagree about the state of the world, and do that in ways that are respectful—to be able to hear differing views and engage them honestly and respectfully. If you can't hear somebody else's take on an issue, why are you in college? The third one is empathy. I want to avoid and alleviate suffering; I want people's suffering to be less. This is what motivates me in the world. I don't call things evil anymore. I don't say Republicans are evil. I say those policies are going to increase suffering. I don't say we have to fight climate change. I say if we don't do this, more people will suffer. If we have more guns, more people are gonna suffer. I find that's very disarming because nobody wants to defend suffering. But for me, this approach is based in empathy. Whatever the issue is, right, I'm trying to go to that point of empathy and compassion. The ability to hear oppositional ideas and worldviews and engage them respectfully. Go into the world and try to alleviate suffering as best you can.

Anthony: It seems to me there's something about the classroom that we often miss because we are so committed to the idea that the classroom is a safe space. And what we mean by that is, the professor will only say things that students are comfortable with. Right? However, I think the classroom is really a space of challenge, of transformation, of new ways of approaching difference, not as a problem to solve but as an opportunity. And it seems to me that this is one of the lessons that the larger humanist community needs to learn: These conversations, these confrontations, ought to make us better.

Phil: Yep, I hope so. I agree with you. I agree with you. Absolutely. That's how we grow.

Anthony: Yeah, yeah. And here's the thing for me, Phil. You're in this environment that is secular, and you're encountering students who are open to this sort of challenge. Right? And you said out loud what many of us humanist in the academy only thought. Dammit, we need secular studies! How did you get to that point?

Phil: Okay, there were a couple of things happening simultaneously that all just kind of jelled. So, the first one I already mentioned. I started teaching a class on secularism and skepticism; the student response was huge. Their eyes were lighting up, their minds were lighting up, and they were so moved and blown away by learning about religion from this perspective, and learning about secularism as an alternative worldview. At the same time, I was always going to religious studies conferences, where I found a few other colleagues who were noticing that atheism was starting to explode with a growth in the religiously unaffiliated. And what they were writing and studying was somewhat marginal at these meetings. What are we studying? We didn't have the language. We didn't have the concepts. We didn't have the taxonomies. We didn't have the typologies. What does it mean to be nonreligious? Who are nonreligious people? What do we know about their voting behavior, their demographics, their child-raising? There was a kind of recognition that as social scientists—whether we're psychologists, anthropologists, sociologists, you name it—there's a huge chunk of humanity that we're not really talking about. It's a kind of residual category. There might be some survey about how often you have sex and it's by religious affiliation, and then the last category might be nonreligious. But who are most people? Are they differentiated in any way? I started to realize there are colleagues out there who are wanting to study nonreligious people, secular people, secular culture. And while my class tended to be a critique of religion, there was this more affirmative study of secular life. It wasn't about debunking religious claims, or promoting skepticism. I had local colleagues interested in this type of work and were teaching courses on secularism. So, we decided to propose a field group, which is what other institutions might call a department. We met on a Saturday. We had a bunch of whiteboards, chalkboards, and blackboards, and we put together classes we taught and classes we'd like to teach. We wrote a proposal that was rejected the first time. It was revised and approved, and we got a secular studies program. And while all that was happening, Barry Cosman had just founded the Institute for the Study of Secularism, Society, and Culture back at Trinity College. Things started happening. The Secularity Research Network in England started having conferences; now there's a *Secularism and Nonreligion* journal online. Things just snowballed from there. But for me, there were two motivations. One, I realized my fascination with religion was decidedly secular in orientation, and I wanted a space for that. And number two, I realized that we just don't know enough about secularism and humanism throughout history, in social politics, in the media, in our world. And so secular studies said, let's take that as the focus of our work. You know, the debunking is fun, but it's not an academic enterprise that's gonna sustain over time. It can get kind of tiresome after a while, but learning more about how secularity intersects with race, class, gender, and sexuality is wide open and exciting to see.

Anthony: There was a tremendous amount of positive buzz concerning secular studies as you were developing it—national buzz, international buzz. But I'm wondering if there was any pushback.

Phil: Yes, there was, and there is. I would say some of it is justified, and some of it is unjustified. One, Pitzer is a small little college. So internally, I would say that I had one colleague who was opposed to secular studies because he thought it was too ideologically driven. He thought we should not have majors at a liberal arts college that have such an agenda, such a perspective. And I think there's some truth to that. I think he's absolutely right. That said, my response was, well, look at the courses we're offering, look at the requirements for the major. We require that students take two or three religious studies classes as part of their secular studies program. Look at the classes we're offering. These are not all framed by an embrace of atheism. Much of the work is critical of atheism. But the bigger thing I noticed was that people just didn't quite understand it. What is it? Why is there a need for it? Why isn't it just part of religious studies? So, the bigger challenge we had was not that people were opposed to it, but that people just didn't understand it. And I think that's a very important challenge. There's also the push for a clear sense of the pay-off of a course of study. What is the point of secular studies? What does it offer? How does it contribute to a broader understanding of the human experience? And that's an important task and challenge to take on.

Anthony: So, answer this question for me, Phil. Fill in the blank: higher education is better with secular studies because . . .

Phil: Because you cannot understand much of the world if you don't understand secularity and secularism. You can't understand what's going on in India right now, Turkey, Israel, the United States, if you don't understand that nonreligious people, nonreligious movements, have been part of humanity since recorded history and are a growing presence in the world today. For the first time in history, we have a majority of people in certain societies who are nonreligious. In Estonia, in Scotland, in the Netherlands, more people are saying they're nonreligious than are. We have more nontheists in Norway than theists. This is a sea change. So, what I would say is we need secular studies in higher education because nonreligious people and nonreligious movements are a significant element in politics, in the media, in popular culture.

Anthony: Last question for you, Phil. And I want to ask this question in light of what we both know is taking place in higher education. There are two parts to this question. First part, what do you see as the future of higher education, particularly the liberal arts? And what is the future of secular studies?

Phil: You're getting me on a bad day, Tony. I'm pessimistic about the future of higher education and the liberal arts. I'm not going to blame religion. I'm going to blame our capitalist world system here. But students are concerned with employment options after college, and they are selecting a course of study in light of that concern. I can't blame them. There are economic realities out there. My fear and worry are that students are more and more going to be concerned about their economic viability. So, I'm pessimistic about the future of higher education and liberal arts. I feel like it's more and more going to be a privilege of the wealthy elite. When you look at how much education is costing, it's insane. In terms of the future of secular studies, I'm on a wait-and-see basis. There was a big flurry ten years ago, but it doesn't seem like other secular studies departments are going to pop up, but I hope I'm wrong. I hope I'm wrong.

PART II

Human Creativity

5

"The Afrofuturistic Gardener"

Angelbert Metoyer

Anthony: Today we have with us a good friend and a tremendous artist, Angelbert Metoyer. His bio starts with his age, but I'm not going to reveal that because if I tell his age, then he's going to try to tell my age, and we're gonna have problems. And he's my brother from another mother, so we can't afford to have problems. So, suffice it to say he is an American visual artist at the forefront of Afrofuturism. He began his artistic career through Rick Lowe's Project Row Houses in Houston, Texas, and held his first solo exhibition there in 1994.[1] He subsequently moved to Atlanta to study drawing and painting at the Atlanta College of Arts. Although a bit of a nomad having lived in various parts of the world, Angelbert currently splits his time between Houston and Rotterdam. His art explores memory and social history through the lenses of science, philosophy, and religion. He makes use of a wide range of artistic materials. And his work is in the permanent collections of the US Department of State, we won't hold that against him, the Museum of Fine Arts—Houston, the Charles H. Wright Museum of African American History, the African American Museum of Contemporary Art, and a host of other museums. I'm honored to call him friend. Angelbert, let's start this way. Give us a sense of when you knew you're a visual artist.

Angelbert: When I knew I was a visual artist—well, making things hit me early, and I've never done anything else. But I started calling myself an artist around the age of thirty-six. And it was really because I had kind of a multi-interest in terms of what I would discipline myself to focus on at any time. And it got to the point where I would just say I was an artist because of my kind of interest in the kind of things that I could build in terms of color seeking; you know, seeking material. But I've never done anything else other than make what I envision—seeking it, creating it, you understand? So, again, I would say I started calling myself an artist in my thirties. But drawing, painting, sculpting, making sound were all encouraged by my parents from a young age. My parents let me have that space for myself.

Anthony: Hold up a second. It wasn't until your thirties that you called yourself an artist. What were you prior to that? What were you prior to that point when you said, Ah, I'm an artist? How would you describe yourself? If I were hanging out with 25-year-old Angelbert in a coffee shop, and asked you what you are, how would you have responded?

Angelbert: I probably would have said, I do nothing. Or, I would have said whatever I was working on in the moment. So, if I was painting intensely, I would say, I'm a painter. If drawing intensely, I'd say, oh, I'm a draftsman. If making things like the mirrors you see behind me, I'd say, oh, I'm a scientist. I was really basing it on these really small focuses. I'm working on sound, oh, you're a musician, right? But I'm not a musician, because a musician takes on a different level of discipline and a different level of focus. So, it made sense to say that I was a sound artist, you know, because everybody around me were actually musicians, and were informing that work. But it was also making what I was doing in terms of drawing and painting stronger. You understand? When I reached a point where the sonic works were able to fill the atmosphere of my work space, simultaneously I had created a palette of sound and tools I could work from in place. Like lucid dreaming, I was able to control and administer the practice for visualizing the intricate response and render them from the language of my spirituality. Over the years, I realized that this was extremely confusing for others and for myself. And that's when I would say I was an artist, when I started to actually use that as a description of my work. I noticed that artists describing themselves as artists worked. It worked for any discrepancy in my personality or in the things I was describing.

Anthony: But there's an element of this that I'd like to linger over for a minute. Tell me if this is right, because I'm trying to wrap my mind around this. So, 25-year-old Angelbert, sitting in the coffee shop with me, describes himself based upon what he's doing in the moment—a very different sense of time, and how you occupy time. Yes? 30-something-year-old Angelbert is thinking in terms of a longer sweep of time. Yes? Right? And so, if you look at all of those individual moments—I'm painting this day. It's music this day. It's sculpture this day—25-year-old Angelbert is saying, oh, let's just talk in terms of the moment. Yeah?

Angelbert: Yeah, that's definitely it. Because a 22-year-old Angelbert still thought he was a race car driver, and would say that to people: I'm a racer; I'm a race car driver. But you know that didn't go well? Actually, no, it didn't go well at all. So, yeah, I was able to see the moment. And I started spending more time outside of the places where I was comfortable—in terms of college, Atlanta, New York, Houston, California. When I started to spend even more time outside of the States, it became clear to me that my breadth of work and my span of life up to that point said I was an artist. But the moment I started that journey, everything created an alignment.

Anthony: I want to get at something. And I want to get at it in a variety of ways. First, like this: it seems to me, and I don't want to put words in your mouth, that your art, whatever form it takes, whatever materials you're using, there is something about the work that is value driven, and this is trying to make art materially real through a certain set of moral and ethical values. For example, I remember at one point you telling me that there was some good work being done in the community. So, you gave your money without any consideration of what you would do without that money. We're not talking about a few dollars. There are ways in which, it seems to me, your art expresses a certain range of values; but you feel compelled to live that out as well. Yeah? So, talk a bit about how that moral and ethical vision developed over the years.

Angelbert: I think the moments you're bringing up are fascinating moments. Several friends of mine have made the statement that I don't make plans. They're like, oh, you never plan things well. But it's interesting because in that kind of state of being in-between things, sometimes things make themselves clearer for me. During that period of time, I wasn't working. But it was literally like, oh, if we only had this amount, then we could do that with this project. Or if we only had this, we could finish that thing. And it would literally be like, I'm walking down the street and get a text. I read the text, and it's someone saying that they are going to buy my art at the price asked for. And that's exactly the amount of money this organization or this group in the community needs. For me, it was about my silence; I was gaining strength through silence of anonymity—doing something that few people knew about. But it made a huge difference for all the people who needed it. I needed the silence, and they needed the resources. I was trying to gain more capacity.

Anthony: Name the values that were in play—drill down. What were the moral or ethical values that drove you to do that? Was it you trying to live in light of a certain range of moral and ethical values that were reflected in what you produce and in how you touch the world? Or, was it just home training?

Angelbert: Yeah, that kind of ask-in-silence-and-receive-openly type of idea. You know what I mean? I noticed that there was a tangible value that was far beyond the abstract value. I can't explain it. Yes, it's a part of childhood training, you know what I'm saying—to whom much is given much is required—tithing kind of concept. It wasn't that I was seeking the sense of belonging by giving. I wasn't seeking a sense of connection. I started to realize that those things for me, at that point in my life, were true. I was being raised with my grandmother's wisdom. You understand? Everything she said to me had supergravity because she'd been here for 100 years. And she'd seen it.

Anthony: Let me get at it another way. It seems to me, if you think in terms of your actions, your productivity, what you create, and how you interact, there's something about it that speaks an interest in transformation or redemption. There's a value judgment in there, right? And I say that in part, because what sticks out for me is the material you use and the way you describe the materials. There's something poetic about it. And by poetic, I mean, a kind of destruction that frees material to tell a different story. You take these materials, and you work them against themselves and allow them to tell another story that's related to people who have been marginalized and disregarded. With your art, it seems to me, you're reconstituting the memory, the cultural memory, the personhood, the history of people who have been marginalized and disregarded. Does that make sense?

Angelbert: That's definitely on par. Because it wasn't like I was staying within this kind of realm of art to do that. When I think about that, I did go far to do this work. I was looking at and using what you might call the excrement of the industry—taming my chaos and offering something different.

Anthony: That raises a question for me: How does this interest in redemption and transformation as a value that transcends time and place work out? Give me a sense of how that works out in terms of your artistic production. What's your process?

Angelbert: In my youth, and my younger years, I was bringing imagery into my work from my dreams. Once I began calling myself an artist, my thoughts transformed and I began to think and work based on visions. In a way, my process is really about materials. I'm working with the materials to mutate the materials. Before, I would be aggressively working, and now I feel like I'm gardening—tending to things, like watering plants, fixing hedges, and building up leaves that become the mulch for building another thing. So, my use of materials looks to reflect the cycle of life—like you would see in a garden. That has helped me to create more deliberately.

Anthony: Do you think curators and collectors sense this process in your work?

Angelbert: I think curators have a job, a vision, and a mission that belongs to institutions and reflects their own self-discovery. But for me, there's an aspect of the work where I have to be still. It's about being still inside one's space and tuning everything else out. You can think about it like the "prayer closet" idea. The transformation or redemption involves me not utilizing what's popular or typical. Instead, I try to embrace the garden idea and connect with creation and with history—a John Coltrane experience, or even a Jimi Hendrix one.[2] The cool thing about Jimi Hendrix is that he was able to do that on the stage, more than he did it in his studio. On the stage, he was a creator—if you really look at him as an artist, and not as a musician. He's writing; he's building music. But on the stage, there's a whole other thing that's unplanned, because the stage is more his garden. His stage is my studio.

Anthony: Yeah, something about your comments reminds me of your piece, "Icon Execution". Anyway you mentioned Coltrane. And you mentioned Hendrix. And I would agree with you. But isn't there also another element there in that this sort of creativity, this sort of rebellion, comes with costs? What has been the cost for you?

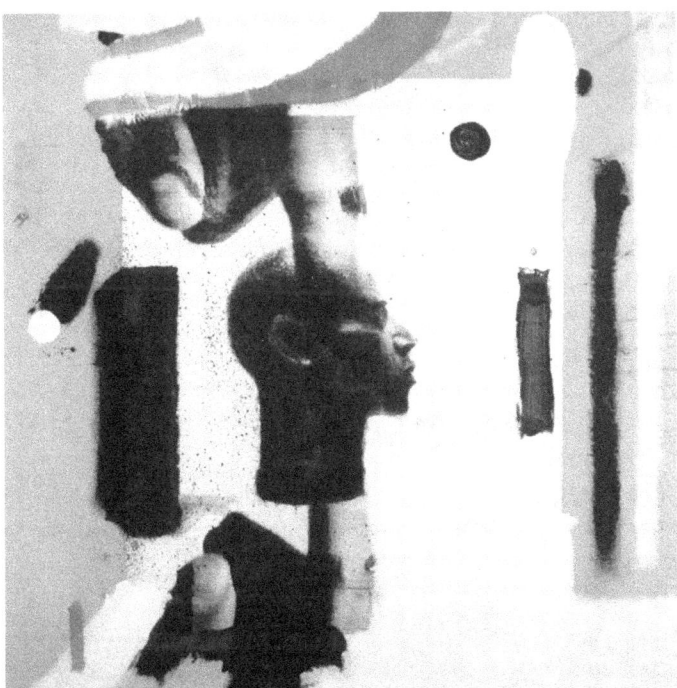

FIGURE 5.1 Icon Execution, *Coal dust, oil, and paper on canvas, 2010.*

Angelbert: Everything. They were consumed by the process; they lost themselves in the process.

Anthony: You have not? Have you lost yourself? The flip side of this creativity is the potential for destruction. And I would say that on one level within your art this is where the Afrofuturism comes in; there is a kind of tension that can be uncomfortable for the viewer. It's a tension between redemption and destruction, possibility and demise. And it seems to me within your art the way to remain somewhat intact is to be transformed. Right? You and your work—Coltrane and Hendrix—involve embodied bodies, but they're not necessarily the type of embodied bodies we're used to seeing walk down Main Street. They are bodies that reflect a push against the traditional boundaries informing how we occupy time and space. Does that make some sense? Yeah, I'm gonna take that silence as a "no."

Angelbert: No, it's not that it doesn't make sense. If I'm tending to the garden, and I'm here for a short while, I'm not going to judge what is created, but I will learn the name of the creation. I'm tending to them. If a vision of a drawing comes to me or painting comes to me, and if I make it, it's going to be fast because I saw every aspect in that vision. My work is like a rehearsal. I'm sitting. I'm present to help it to be birthed.

Anthony: Unpack that for me.

Angelbert: I've looked at some of my images and said, 'whoa, who can live this?' When I look at a painting that I've worked on for decades, and I know underneath all of those layers is something possibly hideous to someone else. But the process of me using the materials has adorned and recreated that image. But I know what's under it. And I know that the thing that's under it has been transformed and also subdued. And so, it's a part of the power of the object, instead of being ruled by the object.

Anthony: Let's drill down a bit. I've had the good fortune of being in your studio. I know something about your work; I've written about your work, but most of those reading this haven't been in your studio. So, let's take one particular piece and discuss it in relationship to what you've been saying about your process and vision.

Angelbert: There is a work that I think is, for me, a type of foreshadowing. And the work itself was from a really quick vision I had when I was 21 years old and on an airplane. I started sketching on some paper, and it was just a group of thirteen images. They were insects, animals, and shapes. It started to seem like what I was doing was gaining velocity. Even after getting off the plane and going to bed. Immediately the next day I went into the space I was working in, and I started the drawings on a larger scale. I started to assemble them the way I saw them in my dream. The first one was a piece called the "Face of God." It was made up of a double-headed creature, and it was one of the first times I created one of these unattractive creatures. I put it on top of a pedestal—a throne, so to speak—and underneath it was a bull. The eyes at the top of the piece were made from two dogs that were kind of hovering above this creature. But when you stand back, it literally looks like a face with a beard. And then that piece led to unlocking the "Face of God," and I created another piece called "God's Arkestra."[3] "God's Arkestra" had the same creatures that were not visible in the "Face of God" drawing, because that was more of a drawing. And it became this painting made up of literally almost everything I'd saved for myself that I was like, "This is good," I'm not selling it. I ended up cutting up those works and constructing a map. There was a giant world inside of this composition. And that was called "God's Arkestra." In making it, I started to investigate the connection of my spirit: What is it that I really know? What's underneath and behind my beliefs? That's what I focused on—aspects of the portrait of me in that painting. But if you look at the entire composition, it was so abstract that you could tell there was no gravity. The entire thing was made without gravity. And it was like light. It was the idea of light but not a light bulb—luminescence coming from the lack of gravity. It was the light of weightlessness.

Anthony: Really interesting. Say more.

Angelbert: I started diving into trying to make this portrait and slowly I created a picture of myself. When I was a kid, I had a dream that involved a giant bear. I ended up having this dream with my father, where the bear finally came into my home. My father told me to tell it to leave. I didn't, because I was like, it was destroying all my enemies, right? If a kid at school picked on me, I'd dream about the bear eating the kid. The power that is my mind cleared a path for me to make my work. When I started to have these dreams and make these images from my dreams, I started winning awards, and getting opportunities to travel abroad and compete for prizes. This is how I met people like Rick Lowe, Michelle Barnes and Jesse Lott.[4] These local people in Houston opened up more opportunities for me to focus and expand my work—this connection between dreams (dreamscapes) and a type of realism, and a form of futurism tied to ancient mystic feelings.

In 2003, I finished the final piece of this trilogy I mentioned. The final piece was a self-portrait called "Map for entering and exiting the body." Then what

FIGURE 5.2 Black Devil in Berlin, *Coal dust and graphite on artist washed paper, 2014.*

I did was take this giant piece "God's Arkestra" and this other giant drawing called "Face of God," and I imposed it into my body—revisited the figure of me wearing the bear skin, on my body. In my forehead I had a rhinoceros tusk, as depicted in some Senufo sculpture.[5] I gave myself a kind of intense mouth because my whole thing was "nothing ever goes wrong." I gave myself this mouth that I didn't want to open. I went back, and I revisited that drawing as a "Map for entering and exiting the body."

Anthony: One of the first pieces I saw of yours was "Black Devil in Berlin", and that raised important questions for me. We got to some of those questions in other conversations. But what you are saying here I need more information concerning. I need to understand this. I need to wrap my mind around it. There's something about this particular piece that involves the subconscious being expressed. Help me understand the project you just described.

Angelbert: The realization of those three works became for me a type of "on earth as it is in heaven" concept. This heaven in my mind is either achievable, or it's already here.

Anthony: It strikes me that you're not just privileging the subconscious. Right? You're not saying the expression of the subconscious is what really matters? It seems there is too much attention to what is taking place within the context of the social world for that to be the case. There's too much that expresses relationships—family and community—that expresses race and anti-Black racism for you to be concerned simply with the subconscious.

Angelbert: I think that's because that is what the subconscious is processing. I'm in my dreams, bringing this dream into reality in order to process it. When it comes out, it's coded in my way of understanding myself in it, not to separate myself from it, but to see myself in it. I am wearing the skin of my protector. I am fitted with things to protect my mind. I'm also fitted with eyes to see exactly where I should go. And my ears are covered with the ears of another animal, to hear the things that I need to hear, to move a certain way with the eyes. My hands are fitted; my feet are actually the feet of a creature. I have this nervous and uncomfortable disposition for the feet of a frog. Like, it can't! But there's something about the frog. I also kept realizing that every level of discretion that became apparent to me was also a part of my gravity and my silence. There's no gravity, but these things create gravity for me.

Anthony: Folks come and see your solo exhibits, your shows. They walk in a certain way, thinking about the world in a certain way, moving through the world in a certain way—either explicitly or implicitly moving in relationship to a certain set of values and moral codes. Do you want them to leave differently? What do you want people to get out of experiencing your art? How should they be different as a consequence of having experienced your art?

Angelbert: I really look at what I'm doing now as more of a medicine. I am not that interested in beautifying someone's house as much as I'm interested in giving them something that gives them power. Understand? There's something intensifying, something repelling, and there's some people who want that. I see that those people who live with those more challenging objects have a different sense of how they operate in the world. You know what I'm saying? Like the people who live with the more challenging objects seem to have a stronger capacity for their movement and shared reality, especially in their purpose. Other people want the thing that's beautiful. It's more about adorning their space and their presence.

Anthony: Let me stop you right there for a second because you're being very nice. So let me push a little and I'll push this way: I get what you're saying, but I also understand that on more than one occasion you and others have described your work as representing Afrofuturism. And you can think about Afrofuturism as a mode of rebellion.[6] It is a way of thinking and creating that which is determined to understand Black life as not being wiped out by anti-Black racism. In a word, Black life and Black people are in the future. It seems to me this is a really bold statement concerning your work. Think about your work as being related to Afrofuturism.

Angelbert: Man, Tony, it's so funny. There's so much space around why I do things. Like I said, the core of my work is experiences from my youth that I hold in place, and they are so intense. I'm living out a script, almost, you know? I feel like I'm living the background of that painting "God's Arkestra"—how I built that painting outside of the images that show you what's going on in the future. And so, for me all of that begins with these meditations that I would have, where I felt like I was in contact with a future descendant of mine—seven million years into the future. It's almost impossible to conceive: Will we even have a sun seven million years into the future? But the place—I've seen it; I've experienced it all through meditation and dreaming—that's been a part of my reoccurring dream since childhood. And I think that's what keeps me going as an artist—keeps me in that frame of creativity. And the thing that I made is a talisman to the person who stewards it.

6

A Serious Sense of Play

Jamal Cyrus

Anthony: I've been looking forward to this conversation with Jamal Cyrus for some time now. For those who don't know, he received his Bachelor of Fine Arts from the University of Houston and his Master of Fine Arts from the University of Pennsylvania. He is an award-winning artist, who recently received the prestigious Driscoll Prize.[1] His work explores the forgotten or fragmentary accounts of African American culture and identity. He raises clear questions about history—what is overlooked and why, and the biases held by those writing and interpreting human experience. In his art, he uses a range of materials, including musical equipment and clothing, and he transforms them. He has participated in national and international exhibits, including "Day for Night: 2006 Whitney Museum of American Art Biannual," shows at the Station Museum in Houston, the Menil Collection in Houston, and the High Museum.[2] This is a small bit of your background, but could you say more concerning your personal history?

Jamal: I grew up in Houston, Texas. Yeah, "Htown." I come from a family, primarily on my mother's side, of musicians—gospel musicians. So, art and creativity were always important aspects of my life—but primarily music. I never had the tenacity to learn an instrument, but I was good at drawing and I was kind of interested in visual art, so that was the way I decided to go creatively. And luckily, there was support for it. I grew up primarily in Missouri City—the Sugar Land area—in the suburbs. I was embedded within my Black family, but outside of that, because of the area, I was exposed to a diverse group of cultures. I would skateboard when I was younger, and I listened to what they called New Wave music,[3] but rerouted myself back into Black culture, socially through Hip Hop that was being made in the late 1980s and early 1990s, such as De La Soul, A Tribe Called Quest, KMD, and others.[4]

There's this thing within my work about music, relating to its functional aspects within Black culture outside of it being entertainment. It was a way of building community, a way of identity formation, used to distribute political messages, and all that. After high school, I went to Texas Southern University and was exposed to the philosophy of Dr. John Biggers, which was really impactful. The professors there gave me a foundation for what I would build on later.[5] However, I didn't graduate from Texas Southern; I ended up graduating from the University of Houston. But I do feel like my understanding of what art is and does comes from those experiences at Texas Southern.

Anthony: Could you say more about the artists beyond John Biggers who have influenced and informed your work?

Jamal: Yeah, so, in high school we had a class in art history; but we weren't really exposed to many artists within the Black Arts tradition—or really artists of color in general. It was just primarily European modernists. So, my main experience in terms of finding out about the history of art and connecting it to myself comes from Texas Southern. Taking Dr. [Alvia] Wardlaw's African American art history course let me connect the dots between Africa and some of the things that were going on in the United States.[6] The artists that were really important for me at that time were people like David Hammons, Project Row Houses with Rick Lowe, Jesse Lott, Jean-Michel Basquiat, and Beyte Saar. Let's see who else: some of the Harlem Renaissance figures, like Jacob Lawrence. Those people were important to me and started to create in my mind a visual vocabulary, and approaches to race I pulled from for my own work.[7]

Anthony: I think folks move from doing to being. Let me explain. In my own case, I was surrounded by books. My oldest sister was working on a master's degree and then a PhD, so I had a sense of writing. But it took a good number of years of doing stuff, of writing, before I understood myself to be a writer. For some folks, that type of identification is immediate, but not for me. I'm curious. When did you realize you did not simply produce art, but you were an artist?

Jamal: The first artistic medium I really fell in love with was photography. And when I was a teenager, I wanted to be a photographer. But I still hadn't made that connection between art making as being a thing. Yeah, it being a thing, which could really fuel and raise my quality of living, I didn't get that until my second year at Texas Southern. I was probably around nineteen, maybe twenty, when I really began to understand that art making was, at least how I was using art making, a part of my own self-education. I was really getting a reward from my artistic activity, which started with myself and then shared with others. And people were responding favorably, and so that was the moment when I started to see a future in being an artist.

Anthony: You were receiving awards, and art was touching something in you. What were you getting from your art?

Jamal: Growing up in Houston, and still to this day, Texas public schools are notorious for gaps in the history that is taught. So, there were a lot of gaps within my education that I needed to understand and work out. Starting with slavery, trying to understand the more complex histories embedded within slavery, some of which were touched on in the Hip Hop I was listening to, and the movies I was seeing. Around the time I was an undergrad, the movie *Sankofa*, by Haile Gerima, came out.[8] And there was a bubbling up within popular culture that was supporting this kind of research, this kind of direction. That's what I used, and what really inspired me: starting with slavery and then from slavery going to early Black political movements, and, then, from there going to the civil rights movement. I particularly found the Black liberation movement interesting. I was trying to understand the historical direction of Black people in America, and with that leading to a better understanding of myself and my capacity. I think within Black American culture there's always been an active participation with history. It's not just about historical documents; it's also about how those materials help to fuel your sense of identity and your sense of the future. I was looking for that kind of reflection on and positioning toward history.

Anthony: That raises a question for me, and I'm sure it's not an unusual question for you when you're interviewed. What is art meant to do? What is your philosophy of art? The conversation so far has circled around that type of question, but let's address it directly.

Jamal: I would say to beautify, to raise, and to mark. I think there's generally a human need or desire for beauty in our visual world. I think artwork is also used to educate, to raise the consciousness, to inspire, whether on a personal, political, or sacred level. And then art is also used to commemorate people or events. At least within my own work, those are the elements I try to activate, maybe not every work but, ideally, they all work on some level to beautify, to mark, and to commemorate. I think that has to do with knowing that you are part of an artistic tradition, right? You might want to engage with that and

FIGURE 6.1 *Misconstrued Rap Lyric #1, Triple beam balance, painted plaster bust of D. Martin Luther King, shelf 20 × 19 × 6 inches, 2019.*

expand that. In my work, I'm trying to also understand more intimately what the unique formal qualities of Black art are. What makes it so evocative? I often start with music and sound, but the visual is there as well.

Anthony: I get what you're saying concerning these three markers. But I wonder if there's a distinction to be made. Do Black artists have an obligation that isn't present in the work of the dominant population? W. E. B. Du Bois, for example, said art has to be political—has to do political work; it has to do some heavy lifting.[9] Do you see Black art having obligations that aren't shared?

Jamal: Well. I don't know if I would use the word obligation. I wouldn't want artists to think that they are obligated to work with their social reality, although I do feel like that is where some of the most impactful work comes from. It may not deal with that experience directly, but it's able to fuse and transform that experience in other ways through the visual world as well as sonically. But I wouldn't even want to use the word "obligation," because there is, even within the Black Arts Movement, that connection made between being representational and being socially engaged.[10]

Anthony: I'm an outsider. I am not an artist in the same way. But let me into that world for a minute. Can you give me a sense of artist intent? How do artists determine how much of themselves they put out there and how much they hold back? Once it's in the museum or gallery, viewers weigh in. But, again, what is the role of artist intent? Does that make sense?

Jamal: That does make sense, but how to explain it? You know, it's on an artist-by-artist basis—particularly if you're talking with Black artists. There's sometimes a frustration with thinking that they have to work with certain types of content—or being pressured to work with that type of content to be successful. That's on the part of the Black community and white expectations. Right? Sometimes there is resistance to that. I was actually just talking to my wife this morning a little bit about this, and the desire for the post-Black within Black visual arts. Again, we have to think about this on the individual level, but I do feel that in some cases, like in Master of Fine Arts programs, sharing traumatic histories with white professors and a white student body can be difficult, so they shy away from doing that.

Anthony: I want to acknowledge that there's something unfair about my question: "Jamal, speak for ALL Black artists." It's like "Tony, your Black . . . speak for all Black people! Tell us what ALL Black people think!" So, let's drill down and just talk about you. It seems to me, to the degree I'm familiar with your work, there are values you bring to your work and values you try to exhibit through your art. What are some of the values that you bring to your art, and what are some of the values you try to express through your art?

Jamal: I do feel that within my work right now I'm trying to come to a fuller acknowledgment of important people and events within Black American culture. What is the makeup of Black American culture? What are the philosophies, people, and influences shaping its makeup, its nature—that give its peculiarity? I think there is a typical way of approaching that subject, and I'm trying to get outside of that. I'm trying to understand the principal aesthetic elements at play within Black American visual art—those are the things I'm trying to highlight and value. I would say, it's difficult because I wasn't exactly trained to do this work in regards to identifying formal parts of the Black visual tradition. It's very difficult in terms of understanding and isolating the things that really fuel Black visual art versus how people are trained to think about Western art, you know?

Anthony: You know I have to push this a little bit. So, when I write I'm in conversation with certain folks because I can get with their view of the world. As I write, I can get with Alice Walker because I appreciate the way in which she thinks of the human in a larger arrangement of life. I can get with Du Bois because I understand and appreciate his sense of the dynamic of race as an ongoing concern and problem, right? I can get with Richard Wright because he surfaces for our attention the messy and uncomfortable dimensions of life. So, when you're creating, who are some of the folks who speak to you—folks you can get with? And what is it about their values that speaks to you?

Jamal: I think about this idea of creating works that speak on multiple levels. So, whether you talk about the spiritual, or you talk about the spatial, or you talk about the aesthetic, the artists I gravitate toward are able to create works that speak to all of those levels. For instance, Southern vernacular art has been really important for me, probably for the last five to ten years or so. My mentor, Terry Adkins has been important to me because of the type of work he produced.[11] So, a lot of the artists that I use as directional, like how you mention Richard Wright and Alice Walker, are this group of artists who come out of the late 1970s.[12] Their work is abstract in terms of form, but they use history and materials to try to address the Black experience—but stake out new territory formally as well.

Anthony: It seems to me that one of the values expressed in your work is of tremendous importance; it's one of the principles that animates your work and it's the sense of an identity grounded in history and materiality. You're concerned with the integrity of Black identity. If that's right, tell me more about it. If I'm wrong, well, tell me that.

Jamal: Integrity? What do you mean by integrity?

Anthony: I mean that you are dissecting the popular narrative of the United States—and you are finding our people in that process. You're asking, who's been forgotten? Right? For me, that speaks to not only the identity of Black people but also the integrity of the people. You aren't content with the dominant narrative, but you are finding us elsewhere in the story.

Jamal: Honestly, I have not thought about it in this way. So, you're helping to push me. Even today, in some regards, I've been situated on the margins of Black American culture. Right? I mentioned earlier that as a teen I was involved with things that people considered white—in terms of what was expected from Black youth and what was acceptable in the South. I found myself outside of those expectations. And on top of that, in the early 1990s, I made a conversion to Islam and that also set me on the outside of my family and on the margins of Black culture—at least southern Black culture.

FIGURE 6.2 Pride Frieze-Jerry White's Record Shop, Central Avenue, Los Angeles, *2005–17 collage on album cover, acrylic paint, plywood, wax, plexiglas 121.24 x 126.5 x 12 inches.*

Anthony: That isn't unfamiliar to me in that my people come from North Carolina and Virginia, and they moved to Buffalo, New York, with those cultural sensibilities intact. So, what you're saying makes a lot of sense to me. Within your work, there seems to be on the level of ethics—that is, what we ought to do—an appreciation for disruption. I think in terms of how you force viewers to think sacred and secular together; how you force viewers to think about occupation of time and space in ways that are complex, uncomfortable, yet rich and generative. Is that accurate?

Jamal: Yeah, yeah, it's so interesting. As you said earlier, as creative people, we are placed in these environments, and we respond to these environments—whether positively or negatively, right?

We carry that original cultural moment with us, its impact. I feel like the cultural moment that I was placed in was after the Black liberation movement. This thing, this movement, has been quashed for whatever reason—whether strategic, or whether it's come from inside or outside of our community. It's probably a little bit of both. I'm part of the generation that was trying to figure those things out, as well as trying to stake its claim to our musical tradition. I'm talking about Hip Hop. And it's doing this in a collage fashion, right, where disruption is just part of the makeup. It's disruptive in nature. It's disruptive in terms of the collage aesthetic but, even once it goes out into the world, it's disruptive as well. Right?

I would say I am comfortable with that. I do think it's tailored my sensibility to be what it is. Over time, it's become more subtle and the material I run through this process have become more subtle. But, yeah, I would say that you're right.

Anthony: One of the things I appreciate about your work, as a humanist, is that it isn't heavy-handed. Unlike with John Biggers' "The Upper room" or Romare Bearden's "Conjure Series," you express the religious sensibilities of Black folk without forcing a particular vantage point.[13] You get a sense that religion has mattered, but you call attention to the humans engaged. You urge us to pay attention to the people involved as opposed to the theology involved.

Jamal: Hmm, well, thank you. I think I'm the product of these different approaches to spirituality. I have started to work with an idea of Black religion in terms of the implementation of spirituality within social resistance. And that takes a bunch of different forms. And so, yeah, there's not necessarily a particular religious point of view. I'm just trying to think about the nature of religion, or the interplay between two things—resistance and spirituality.

Anthony: Your work, as I view it, speaks to me on a variety of levels. One of them is the urge to recognize that we are here—and this goes back to what you've said concerning rescuing of our position in history. It urges a recognition that we are here. We are present. It urges us to view our organizations, institutions, and our cultural production. It involves an opportunity to see ourselves as embodied beings moving through the world and to see the significance in that. This is powerful.

Jamal: Thank you. Thank you. Yeah, I make these works to try to clarify my position in the world—to help me with my everyday understanding. And sometimes that comes through. When artists make work from authentic places, I think that can be a very powerful exchange.

Anthony: I have to ask a question that you probably hear many times a week: What is your process?

Jamal: I, at one time, was very much about going into the library, going into the museum, record shopping. All that kind of stuff came into my "research process," as an artist. But since I've moved back to Houston (in 2010), it's been a lot slower and more organic. And things that come into my work,

FIGURE 6.3 Lights from the Garden, *Bentwood chairs, stainless steel rods, oak flooring 74 x 87.5 x 31.75 inches, 2019.*

they end up being experiences that I have day-to-day. And then that becomes connected to what I may be reading or listening to—and I try to create out of that. I'm always in the studio, and sometimes I have a particular idea that I'm working with. Sometimes the work starts with a part of a title, or sometimes it might start with an object. I do a lot of purchasing on eBay. Do you remember seeing the Budweiser posters with African kings and queens on them? So, that's one of the things that I'm working with right now. Sometimes I'm dealing with objects I've bought and use them along with other material. A lot of the stuff that I do is based on play, and it does often involve disruption, as you were saying—like tearing, ripping, taking apart, and putting back together in different ways. When the work is done in a playful manner, it's like you're looking for something, you're looking for the "thing" during the process.

Anthony: This is one of the reasons I highlight values. For example, you take a material and you make it do work it wasn't intended to do. You take denim jeans, and you pull them apart and make something very different. It seems to me in making the art and viewing the art, it's not about the material itself, but what that material can be made to communicate.

FIGURE 6.4 Medicated Shield, *wooden pew, mandingas, sand bags 35.25 x 84 x 23.5 inches, 2021.*

Jamal: Right, right. It's what the material communicates or what has been embedded within the material. And I do think that is very West African—like a sacred object or relic. I think it's also in Southern vernacular art in different ways. One of the things I'm inspired by is that type of artistic approach. And oddly enough it works. There's an exchange on the level of the material that might be shocking, but it works.

Anthony: The idea of the relic or totem is interesting in that it's meant to prompt a certain way of thinking or seeing. So, I go back to your use of denim. Those aren't jeans on the wall. You create a type of dissonance that forces us to ask questions. And this frees us to think differently.

Jamal: Yeah, yeah. That's what I'm trying to create, those types of responses in the viewer. But it is not always a conscious thing on my part. Right? I mean, there may be something I want to get from the material, or an inclination that I get out of working with the material, or something I learn about the material and that I want to use. Just through handling and manipulation of it repeatedly this other thing eventually comes out.

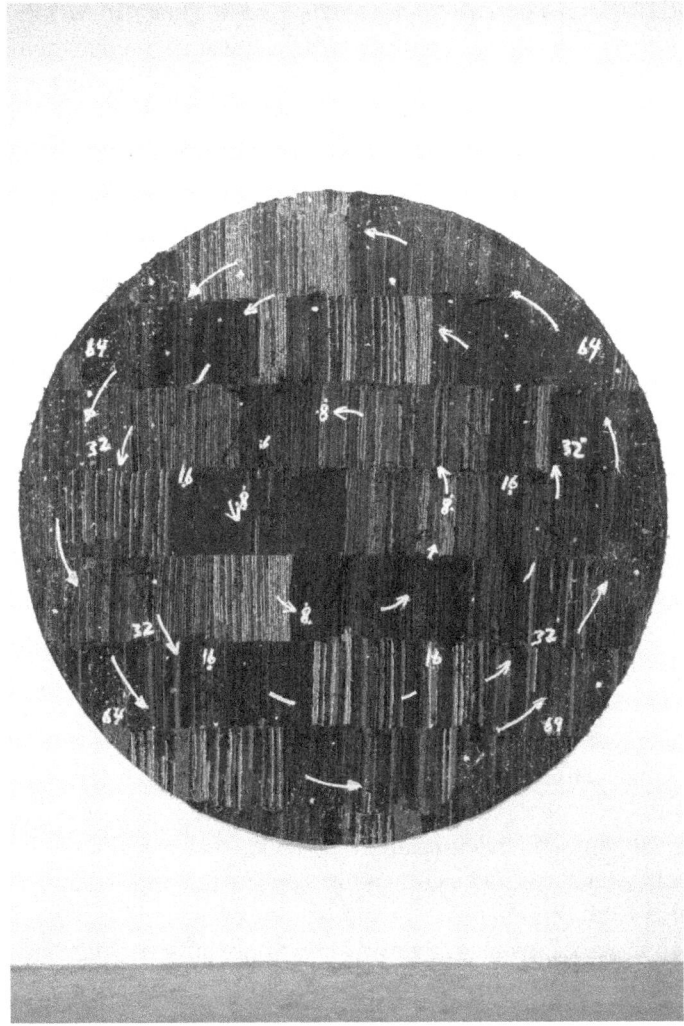

FIGURE 6.5 Inner Necessity to Outer Time (Run Mary Run), *denim, cotton thread, burlap 84 x 84 inchemode_comments, 2021.*

Anthony: Tell me if I'm making too much of this. I'm thinking of pop art, and I'm thinking about Andy Warhol's Brillo Box, which is meant to prompt certain reactions.[14] And it raises questions: What is art? What's the difference between art and the everyday? What's the difference between viewing and using? It seems to me that on some level your art prompts questions as well: What is Black life and what is the value of Black life? I see this in relationship, for example, to your use of history. You take these experiences, these forms—that denim—and you force different considerations. Think about denim and Black bodies. Denim jeans meant work, labor. Dr. Martin L. King, Jr. wore denim jeans during certain campaigns because it meant heavy lifting to be done. Denim can confine the Black body, reduce it to labor, to a mere physicality. But you take denim and force a different range of considerations that urge a rethinking of the bodies that wear denim—to rethink values and the value of Black bodies outside of what they can do.

Jamal: Thank you for that response. Thank you for that. Honestly, I haven't had that take on it. But it's definitely in line with what I'm trying to flesh out in regard to Black American history and that material. There are also the questions about style and the value of the role Blacks have played in this country. It's an open-ended question—but definitely one of the questions that I'm asking when I'm putting those pieces together.

Anthony: For those who are lucky enough to see your work in person, how should they engage it? How should we encounter your work?

Jamal: I think you can enjoy my work just on the level of the visual—what it presents. For the denim works, I create these collages and viewers can talk about tonality, texture and form. I tried to give these works enough attention so that there are those elements present. But I think there are also other layers viewers can dig into. To do this, I would ask viewers to be patient, to go on a journey with me in terms of connecting material to a particular history I'm trying to connect to, figure out, or discuss. A lot of the work contains a functional element, and this is related to the idea that many of the traditional West African sculptures had a certain functionality to them. And so, I am into the idea that what I create has a functional component to it, and that function also relates to our experience. That way I try to get at where they are coming from and why they were made. Again, I would just ask for patience because viewers won't get everything the first time. Good work reveals itself slowly.

Anthony: I have a question, and it's a rather crude question. How long does it take you to go from research to a finished piece—a piece you are happy to show?

Jamal: It depends. Do you know this artist, Trenton Doyle Hancock, from Houston?[15]

Anthony: No.

Jamal: He's primarily a painter, but he does some sculpture as well. He's an interesting guy. I heard a talk he gave, and he basically said that in the studio he tries to have works that operate on different time frames—that require different things from him. Sometimes things are very quick, then there are things that require a medium level of response, and things that take much longer. In my work you get some of that. The denim pieces take a long time. They're very laborious—repeatedly stripping, gluing, ironing. They also take time because some of the denim pieces are based on particular FBI memorandums, and sometimes it also takes a while for me to find one that I want to use for a work.

Anthony: Wait, wait. You said they come from these FBI memorandums. Please say more!

Jamal: Yeah, for many Black activists, and also other artists, there has been this kind of FBI surveillance going on since the 1930s. So, what I often do is go through the FBI Reading Room, which is an online archive, and look for different people I'm interested in. I see if they have a file, and then I go through those files and try to find documents that speak to a particular history. One of the pieces that I finished recently was about Billie Holiday. Who, because of the song "Strange Fruit," comes under surveillance. They were able to take advantage of her drug habit to try to destroy her career. It's a file that has two newspaper clippings of a story about a drug raid that she was involved with, and that's represented in all black denim, with two angular strips. It looks very abstract, but it's actually taken from these FBI memorandums with underlying political content. It's called "Angular Call to Lady Day." You know Gil Scott-Heron did this song, "Could you call on Lady Day? Could you call on John Coltrane? Now 'cause they'll, they'll wash your troubles."[16] So, this combination between these different musicians and this history is a part of this art making. There's the conceptual component that can take a while and then there's the actual making. Sculptures usually come to me a little quicker because there is a kind of collage aesthetic to the sculpture. So, they come a little quicker.

Anthony: Some artists might claim they are simply uncovering what's already there. But for other artists they are imposing something on the material. Are you uncovering or are you imposing?

Jamal: I would probably say a little bit of both. With many of the two-dimensional works, it is uncovering what is there and translating that in a different way—translating into a different material or medium. With the sculptural work, I would probably say it's imposing a certain logic, or making this thing to do something it was not originally meant to do. That's the thing about the collage or the collision, you know, within the sculptures that I think create a certain dissonance for the viewer.

Anthony: One last question for you. Thinking in terms of your work, but also thinking in terms of the larger arena of work, is there something viewers typically get wrong that drives artists crazy? Are there ways in which we completely misunderstand?

Jamal: There's this thing where certain people think it's a game because of what they see in the museum. They start to think, oh, well, maybe I could have done that. But then they hear these long, drawn-out explanations about the intentions of the artist. So, I would say for most people that I know it's not a game. People create from real positions and really put a lot into their work, and are committed to what they do. So, when you go to the museum, don't always have that skeptical take on the art and artists. People also get it wrong when assuming they could have made what they see in the museum. Maybe they could have done that, but they would have done it after years of making previous moves to get to that point. People see in my work simple materials, simple processes, right? But they don't see what it took to get there.

Anthony: People fail to consider what the work generates. So, people look at a Basquiat work and say, "I could have done that." A couple of things—one, you didn't. But secondly, what does it generate? What does it pull from us? What new thoughts does it force us to have? How does it change us? Impact us?

Jamal: Thinking about Basquiat, I don't personally see others who were synthesizing that number and kinds of traditions, histories, and aesthetics. It's very complex. And so, it's interesting to think about him being at the burgeoning of the Hip Hop movement and the creative sensibility coming out of New York at that time. He's a great example of somebody whose work is mistaken by people thinking they could have done that.

Anthony: It seems to me we do ourselves a disservice if we aren't open to what art is communicating, if we don't allow ourselves to be informed and influenced by the values it seeks to speak.

7

Art Imitating Life

Jeremiah Camara

Anthony: Jeremiah Camara, my brother, I'm going to thank you in advance for what I know will be a great conversation. It couldn't be otherwise, because I'm talking to someone who is multitalented—a writer, a filmmaker, director, producer. His first documentary was *Contradiction: A Question of Faith* and then there's *Holy Hierarchy*. His books include *The New Doubting Thomas*.[1]

Jeremiah: Man, I'm looking forward to this, Anthony.

Anthony: We haven't talked in a minute. So, let's start this way. Could you provide a bit of background for context? Who is Jeremiah?

Jeremiah: Well, Jeremiah Camara is a man from Cincinnati, Ohio. I moved to Atlanta in 1996. And when I asked a person their name, they would ask me, "what church do you go to?" I knew right then I had to do something because I was nonreligious at the time, and I still am. I did not come from a religious background. My parents did go to church; they were believers. But I always just felt like there was something else out there. There's just so much knowledge out there that I had to learn, and so I didn't relegate myself to only the Bible.

Anthony: You mentioned a question: "What church do you go to?" Now, we both grew up hearing the related question, "who are your people?" There was a link for folks between those two questions. They told them everything they needed to know about a person—their moral and ethical sensibilities.

Jeremiah: That's right. That's right. I didn't get that question as much here, in Atlanta, as I did back home. Atlanta is big business, and churches are huge business here. You know, we just had prosperity preacher Creflo Dollar saying that he made a mistake with respect to requiring tithing—people giving 10 percent of their income to the church.[2]

Anthony: Did he return the money?

Jeremiah: He didn't return the money to my knowledge. But he said, hey, I don't regret it because I wouldn't have what I have without the tithes. And then there were people who heard what he said, but they said, listen, I've been tithing for all this amount of time, and I'm gonna continue to tithe. There's a real connection here between the pastors and the people that is just unbreakable it seems.

Anthony: Yes, for a lot of people, when you talk about Black people, you out of necessity talk about Black Church. And in your work you wrestle with this connection in a way that is highly critical of Black churches. I want to get to that, but first help me—in terms of context—understand how you got into filmmaking and film production. Did you wake up one day and say, "I'm going to make documentaries?" How did it happen?

Jeremiah: You know, I started doing the slave sermon documentaries.[3] And so, with those slave sermons, I'm up to like episode 51 now. I took about two years off in order to have time to reflect and work on some other things, which we'll talk about later. But I kept getting comments from people with these slave sermon pieces, like, man, you should do a movie! I wasn't thinking about doing a movie. These slave sermon episodes prepared me really well for doing films because I had to do a lot of editing and other things related to film production. So, I thought about it. I'm in Atlanta, and I have been doing these slaves sermon documentaries, and people are kind of encouraging me to do more. That's what actually led me to make my first film. Now with this second film, *Holy Hierarchy*, I was invited to the Interdenominational Theological Center, here in Atlanta, by one of the professors there—Dr. Riggins Earl. Anthony, I know you know Dr. Earl.[4]

Anthony: Yep, I know him well.

Jeremiah: He read my book, *Holy Lockdown*, and asked me to come to the school. This wasn't for credit or anything like that, but he wanted me to come to the school and see how they are preparing people—seminarians. I went there, and stayed about six or seven months. I read all the books—great books—and one of the books that I ran into was *Shades of Freedom*. I think it's by Leon Higginbotham. Man, that book was very tedious because it had a lot of court cases from the 1600s that led to racist notions and precepts. And that led to *Holy Hierarchy*, dealing with the religious roots of racism in America.[5]

Anthony: It strikes me that your work—the production of these documentaries—fills a gap regarding humanism in general and Black humanism in particular. We, humanists, usually make our case through the spoken word and the written word. We talk our history; we talk our values. We write our history; we write our values. But you use a different art form to tell the humanist story. Is that right?

Jeremiah: That's true. I don't know if there was a film that really took a humanist perspective, an atheist perspective, and criticized the institution of the Black Church before *Contradiction: A Question of Faith*.[6] But I'm also a musician, and I've tried that way to make the point, but film intrigued me. When I was going over and evaluating some of my skills that I had with certain slave episodes, I said, you know what, this is doable. Let's try it. I had written books, but we need a film out here. People like films because they are engaging. If your work isn't engaged, Amazon Prime, for example, will pull your film quickly. And so, I've been on Amazon Prime now for about three years, and I've gotten a lot of good feedback. I'm looking forward to the next film. I'm excited, but we are still in a predicament.

Anthony: Unpack that for me.

Jeremiah: Well, you have to read between the lines sometimes. I think Black Lives Matter has ushered in a period of appeasement. And I think that when you look at the economic divide, not much has changed. But the way that you keep people quiet is to appease them. I think that we're being appeased right now. I think it's still segregation. The money is very segregated. I don't see the real power. I see less than 1 percent of Black people owning commercial property. We had this undertaking in Atlanta called Black Wall Street. And I don't mean to be too critical about it, but there was a Black man who bought a bunch of properties. His goal was to have 100 Black retail shops. The problem with that is he didn't consult with the young people. You can't take on a project of that significance without talking to the youth. But, again, I think that Black Lives Matter has ushered in the age of appeasement. Look, for example, at the Super Bowl. Black people pretty much have taken over the halftime show. We are less than 20 percent of the population, yet we're in, like, 97 or 98 percent of the commercials. Blacks win in the commercials but, in reality, we still don't have victories because you're talking about a group of people who run the businesses that have defined the country. So, there's a lot of work to be done. And we need to let people know that this work is going to take dollars, human effort, human sacrifice, human knowledge. Blacks need to understand and appreciate that change won't come by means of miracles, but through human effort.

Anthony: I think you absolutely are right. Race still matters. I also hear you saying that there's a hyper-visibility for Black folks in terms of entertaining the dominant population. But we are somewhat invisible when it comes to control over the infrastructure of collective life.

Jeremiah: That's what we've aimed for. We wanted to be seen. We strive for that. That's what we want. That's what the goal has been.

Anthony: You really think that? You really think all Black folks wanted was to be seen?

Jeremiah: I do to an extent. I know a person right now, and I won't mention his name; but, wow, he wants to be "head Negro in charge." That's all he really wanted. If you have that type of talent, why not take the next step and control that talent? On a larger scale, I don't see Blacks controlling their communities, establishing groups of businesses—controlling their local economies. If more isn't getting done, I question the desire.

Anthony: Let me push a little bit. I would agree with you that Black folks—like everybody else—have been interested in the American Dream, and have attempted to secure the American Dream. You see this effort in our cultural production; you see it in what we have written. You see it in our films. You see it in the visual arts, and so on. But I don't know if we can explain the push of a Frederick Douglass, or a W. E. B. Du Bois, or understand the desires of a Toni Morrison by talking in terms of just wanting to be seen.[7] I want to tie this to your brilliant critique of Black religion in the form of the Black Church. On one level, you're right, there is this interest in being seen. But with the Black Church, it's a desire to be seen in a particular type of way—the politics of respectability. It's a way of being seen that projects us into the public arena and allows white folks to understand us in relation to their own desires and wants. To the extent whites can see themselves reflected in our attitude, we can progress—at a cost. Is that right?

Jeremiah: Absolutely, I hear you on that. It's a matter of moving beyond style with no substance, so to speak. We gotta get beyond that; we've got to get more substantive—substantive in our efforts, goals, and our desires. It takes time, and I understand that. But I think the Black Church is a big uncomfortable pebble in our shoe. You have that pebble in your shoe, you know, you want to take it off, but . . . . I always use this Asian proverb, which says to exist on the spiritual practice that once saved you in the past is to carry the raft on your back after you've crossed the river. We have crossed many rivers. We don't need to carry this raft on our back. And as I've said, all the things that need to be done, and that have to be done, are going to be done by human beings.

Anthony: Let's talk in terms of *Contradiction* and *Holy Hierarchy*. What's the most significant takeaway? So, if folks watch these documentaries and only take away one thing, what should it be? And please, use this as an opportunity to talk about the content of those documentaries.

Jeremiah: Sure. *Contradiction* basically looks at the powerlessness of Black people in light of the abundance of churches in Black communities. Why are there so many churches and yet so many problems in Black communities? My goal, Tony, was not to be condemnatory. I wanted the people to actually write the documentary themselves, and I went to many different cities and I interviewed many, many people. I didn't cherry-pick participants to any degree. And so, the takeaway, or the point, is we know so little about the things in which we are involved. I think that is the basic takeaway from *Contradiction*. We don't know. Instead, we believe because we've been told to believe. If your grandmother is a theist, she can't tell you anything about humanism. She can't tell you what to think about atheism. I found it striking that when you ask people a simple question: "What did you learn today in church?" They can't tell you. And I've been asking that question for over ten years. We just don't get a solid answer. "Well, I learned that God loves me." Really, just that? You go every week, and you've been going for thirty and forty years, what did you learn that you can take and apply in your community to make your community better? I think that was the takeaway in *Contradiction*, and the takeaway in *Holy Hierarchy* was that things happen for a reason. Racism, in many ways, is a ranking system. Back in the 1600s, there were certain court cases that, like stairs, led to this notion of Blacks being inferior to whites. And there were precepts, which are just general rules, which give people their ideas about other people and how to behave around other people. And so, I lay out these cases in order to explain that Black people didn't do anything wrong in the sight of God. We are in this position because of certain things that happened, not because God was displeased with us and put us in a position to be enslaved. So, the takeaway is the importance of seeing and knowing the effect of religion and race on each another.

Anthony: I want to bring up something that came to me while we talked after the *Holy Hierarchy* shoot in Brooklyn. Even the best efforts of the Black Church, for example, are damaged because in order for the Black Church to function, for its theology to make sense, people have to be broken. What is the Church without sinners? And so, it is extremely difficult to highlight more productive values and possibilities when your theology—your self-understanding—is premised on people being broken and inadequate.

Jeremiah: Absolutely. There's a saying: there's a paddle for every ass. And I don't care if you are Black, brown, yellow, male, female, rich, or poor; life has a paddle for you. We want to talk about whites who are born with silver spoons, let me tell you there are more stories about whites who let this silver spoon tarnish. To keep the spoon polished takes a lot of work. There's a paddle for them too. To ask a white person not to be racist is to ask them not to participate in their privilege. You said, Tony, that people are predisposed to check the category of "the other." There are people born in situations that are undesirable, that they had no control over. But let me tell you something. In this life, nobody is going to feel sorry for you. When you go to church and you have these problems, the preacher wants to act like sunshine and shine a ray of light on you so that you go home feeling better. This is not to say people don't have real problems. Again, there's a paddle for every behind. Being a humanist, and a secularist, I'll share what I told my daughter. She called me up one day with all this "woe is me" stuff. And what I told her is what my friend told me many years ago. He said, "you're not the first and you're not going to be the last to have this issue." That is a very adult, grown folk, way of telling you to put your big folk underwear on, keep it moving, roll your sleeves up, and figure out this problem. So, in church, we conflate the beautiful music, the beautiful sanctuary, the other elements of worship, with truth, and we fail to see what's really confronting us. But at some point, Tony, we have to be realistic about the problems that we're facing, and roll your sleeves and solve the problem. Think your way through it. Realize that no matter what happened, you're not the first that it happened to, and you're not gonna be the last. That's a harsh reality, but preachers don't help people confront that harsh reality.

Anthony: It sounds to me like one of the secular values you're highlighting is individual accountability.

Jeremiah: Absolutely, do the work! Listen, Tony, let me put it this way. Now, people might not agree with this, but I think it's true. The best thing I can do for Black people is not to write a book, or make a film. The best thing I could do for Black people is to get myself together. I've hired twenty-two felons. And many of them have gone on to do great things; some haven't. But I have to get myself together, think, and contemplate. I think that's the key. Help others, but get yourself together first. People are watching, and them seeing you get yourself together will influence and help them.

Anthony: Let me ask you this: in terms of *Holy Hierarchy*, much of the conversation revolves not around individual Christians but around communities—and how communities, churches as organizations, produced theologies, doctrines, and ways of behaving that are detrimental. But with a turn to humanism, is it just about individuals getting themselves together or is there a sense of community—a sense of the collective as well?

Jeremiah: There's a sense of the collective as well because no matter how hard I tried to get Jeremiah together, I'm gonna need the help of others. I can't do it alone. Christians tell you—although it is not anywhere in the Bible—they say that God helps those who help others. Right? Human beings tend to help other human beings. I have a few friends who are addicted to drugs, and they get help when they want help. When they want to help themselves, or when they want to stop, they tend to get help.

Anthony: Tell me if I'm wrong, but—and I don't mean this in a derogatory way at all—I hear something of the lift-yourself-by-your-own-bootstraps philosophy in what you're saying. Is that right?

Jeremiah: Tony, it has to be, it has to be! As a social animal, we have to do that. It sounds harsh; it sounds rough; but what other choice do we have? We can ask for help, and we might receive help. But in the meantime we have to do for ourselves. We have to pull ourselves up!

Anthony: Let me go back to something you said earlier. You talked about whites and white privilege. Isn't it precisely the case that we are asking whites to recognize white privilege and reject it? Isn't that part of what we are asking?

Jeremiah: Yes, but are whites really going to reject the economic benefits of their whiteness? I would say that we have put more emphasis on biblical literacy than we have on financial literacy.

Anthony: So, then, what does social transformation actually mean? What does it require of whites as individuals and as a community?

Jeremiah: Let me jump on my band wagon. It starts with religion. They have to recognize that no cosmic force made them special. Once we have that conversation, we can start to mend other fences. We are having an ongoing, national conversation about confederate monuments, but we aren't having a conversation about removing religious iconography that reenforces white privilege on a theological level; we aren't ready! Everywhere you go—churches, hospitals, gas stations, or Walmart! I tell people every day, Jesus is white! People are like, Jeremiah, why would you say Jesus is white. Well, because he's white in Walmart—the largest retailer! Think of all the films, and programs, that present Jesus as white. Perception—the perception is meaningful. What can whites do? Eradicate white religious iconography—and change the perception of who is valuable, socially significant.

Anthony: That's an important point. Within the context of the civil rights movement, for example, Dr. Martin Luther King, Jr., argues that there's more than one way to be dehumanized. You can be dehumanized by thinking too little of yourself (e.g., Black people), but you can also be dehumanized by thinking too highly of yourself (e.g., white people). There's a role that religion has played in this process of dehumanization. Theology has been warped and shifted in order to justify the advancement of whites, and to justify the dehumanization of Blacks. And it seems to me your documentaries speak about this in rather powerful ways. But outside films and documentaries that are sensitive to humanism as an orientation, what do we do about the way in which the larger industry projects Blacks as being indistinguishable from their religious commitments? How many Hollywood films with Black folks *don't* have something in them about religion? What do we do about that orientation?

Jeremiah: It's not about the victory; it's about attention. There needs to be a movement to eradicate certain perceptions. Take Christmas, for example. When a Black child only sees white nativity scenes, what does that say to that Black child subconsciously? Those images reenforce the assumption of white superiority. Tony, there needs to be a discussion regarding superiority and inferiority because you don't have racism without such notions. There is a theological dimension of this at work, which indicates that God favors whites, and Blacks are the children of Ham and cursed to be servants and of less value. This, of course, is biblical nonsense! These notions aren't some sort of divine mandate; they are human constructions—laws and social codes. Racism is tied to law. Apartheid was law. Jim Crow involved laws. White religious iconography that supports ideas of white superiority needs to be outlawed.

Anthony: Here's the sticking point. It's one thing if you lodge that sense of entitlement or superiority within the confines of human laws and policies. That sense of superiority is easy to challenge. But this has been the benefit of religion; it has given that privilege a transhistorical authority, which means a much more difficult to challenge authority.

Jeremiah: Right, there you go. There you go. It's much more difficult to challenge. Whites will need to prove that the Bible actually endorses their claims to superiority—that Jesus was white. But the way the Bible is typically read gives whites a position closer to the divine than darker people—and this gets played out in social interactions and social assumptions.

Anthony: And it's tied to the US narrative and played out through a particular reading of the Bible. But I wonder how many Christians—white, Black, green, yellow; the color does matter—how many Christians actually read the Bible as opposed to getting their sense of the Bible from what the preacher tells them?

Jeremiah: I think most don't read it.

Anthony: So, what's in the Bible is of limited importance. It's the cultural narrative that drives religious sensibilities. The cultural narrative drives religious commitment.

Jeremiah: Yes, but there will be Blacks who will say the Bible depicts Jesus as having feet the color of bronze. Now, I can interpret that many ways. For some, this description means Jesus was Black.

Anthony: I get it, but that interpretation doesn't solve the problem. The color of Jesus doesn't change the fact that the fundamental figure of the Christian faith is highlighted for his ability to suffer. And that for Christians—and for Black Christians this has a particular taint to it—is a desire to measure our well-being through our ability to suffer. When I was growing up, they said, "no Cross, no Crown."

Jeremiah: I remember that saying, and we deal with these sorts of issues in the documentary. But there's the point, that is the hallmark, the ability to suffer. And that means, as a Christian, I will seek a path of suffering. I will see things through a lens of suffering. Church assumes the importance of suffering; church attendance loses meaning if one doesn't see oneself in relationship to suffering—for example, Christlike. But progress requires moving from this position and embracing a counterintuitive approach—counterintuitive to the dominant Christian narrative.

Anthony: This thinking is embedded in the structure and thought of the church. It gets generated through our cultural narrative. Think in terms of films—this idea of working for the benefit of others, redemptive suffering. Films like *Lilies of the Field* or the *Green Mile* advance this redemptive suffering model.[8] But one of the things you accomplish in your films is opportunity to question some of the theological claims we have just assumed to be accurate. And so, I want to end with this question: We want to encourage folks to view your films, but name another film, or documentary, people should check out.

Jeremiah: *Broken Faith* is one to check out. We need comedians to critique this sense of religious suffering—humor is one way into this conversation. I'm working on a film now called *Crutches*. It's humorous, and its humanist. It's about a loyal church member who's trying to free himself from his controlling pastor. The pastor has manipulated him and gotten him to leave his wife and marry a woman he barely knows. What's crazy is that it is based on a true story. We need to point out all the examples of people who embrace the unlikely theological claim as opposed to the more obvious, and likely, human answer.

8

The Raw Truth of Hip Hop

Harry Allen

Anthony: Harry, thanks for making time to talk with me about Hip Hop. Much appreciated! Man, you've been doing this work for a long time—articles, building organizations, and your affiliation with Public Enemy can't be forgotten. Tell me a little about yourself, your early years, and your introduction to Hip Hop.

Harry: I was born in New York City in the early 1960s, to parents who were Costa Rican of West Indian descent. As is often the case, the goal of many immigrants is to get to the suburbs. So that's what my parents did. When I was around eight years old, we moved to Long Island. And it was while we were on Long Island that Hip Hop was starting to make its way. This would have been 1972. So, I got wind of it out there. I can very distinctly remember, one of the older boys in the neighborhood, whose name was Canute, was telling me about this new uptown sound. He recited a few lyrics; he said, "Mickey Mouse is in the house and Donald Duck don't give a . . .," and it was just those lines, and I was captivated. It was also around that time we started having park jams with DJs. I can remember, of course, some of the DJs would play a record and MCs would rap while they're playing—sometimes with an echo sound. Wow!

I would also say, as I often do, that I was prepared for Hip Hop because of being a Black American, a descendant of African people. To my thinking, there were things that preceded Hip Hop that prepared me, and made me ready for it. The very first thing was the centrality of rhythm in our culture. Rhythm is fundamental to Black culture. And it's fundamental in Hip Hop. The orality of Hip Hop is something that echoes throughout Black culture, and so I see

Hip Hop as a kind of condensation and concentration of these earlier kinds of expression.

I'm old enough to remember when Channel 13 advertised this new show called *Sesame Street*. We were all excited about this because it looked like a lot of fun. I remember that they used to have short films that would emphasize a letter of the alphabet or a number, and they would give you a short lesson about it. There was one called Joe and the Junebug, and you can still find this on YouTube.[1] I remember to this day how this thing went. And it starts: "Once upon a time a guy named Joe noticed a Junebug on his toe, put it in a jar and started to go." It goes on and on and on like this. I later realized that this was a form of patter invented by Black people and established by them not only in jazz but it goes even further back to at least the nineteenth century in what was called pattin' juba (also called "hambone"), a form of orality that was rhymed. It involved the speaker pointing out individuals and making fun of them in a kind of like familial way. What you might call a "roast," or freestyling. This was a kind of orality that preceded Hip Hop and rhyming by at least a century, but wound its way into the culture for people who didn't even necessarily know about it. Again, I say my relationship with Hip Hop began as a young person, but it was preceded by the things that were built into my culture.

Anthony: That's really helpful, and it begs the question: What is Hip Hop?

Harry Allen: That's a great, great question. It's one that I think many people think about. And the way I think about it is that a definition of anything is really contextual. It has to do with your framework and what you're trying to do. For example, you could define Hip Hop musicologically. And by that, I mean, in a manner fit for music or cultural scholars. And this would be a very lengthy and technical definition. Not only because one would have to explain rap to people who are specialists, ostensibly—people who've thought about it very deeply and written about it very deeply. You'd have to talk about specific kinds of things that make it part of the panoply of *working sound*. Not only because you'd have to explain that, but you'd also have to explain DJing, B-boying, writing—which is the original name for what many people call "graffiti." Plus, you'd have to explain what connects all these art practices. And as many know, Hip Hop is commonly held to be four practices: emceeing, DJing, B-boying, and writing. Some have even gone and said Hip Hop is *five* practices, and the fifth is knowledge. I consider this incoherent. That doesn't make sense to me. But if you're a musicologist, you might define Hip Hop, very technically, with a very long definition that has to accommodate all of these forms and how they connect to each other. I have two definitions, one that I use very frequently and one less frequently. First, I say Hip Hop is rap music and its associated forms. I think this is a compact definition that's accessible to most people, even if you're not a fan of the culture. If you talk to a housewife from Idaho, or Minnesota, she probably knows what rap music is. She's probably heard it. And if you talked about breakdancing, DJing, or graffiti, she would have a sense of what those things are. She might be offended by them, or think they're not real art or music, but she would at least know what they are. And I feel that's a simple way to kind of talk about these four forms and their connections. You might even have an idea that these are things that are related. So, I think there's a quick and easy way to define Hip Hop.

Anthony: Thank you for that. It raises two related questions for me. First, why this particular form? Black cultural expression is expansive and has developed over an extended period, with various modes of expression. Why did Hip Hop take this particular form and develop during this particular period? And what was it about that period that made Hip Hop so timely?

Harry: I think there are a couple of things that were going on. In terms of why it took this form, it's very interesting: I took a class called "Black Music and Musicians," when I was at Adelphi University, with Professor Andrei Strobert, who is no longer alive. He was a very good jazz percussionist who also taught. I remember him once saying that the scratch often sounded like the *shekere*, the beaded drum. And then he made the *shk-shk* sound of the drum, and then the *shk-shk-shk* sound of the turntable. This really got my attention. To the degree that that's true, it speaks to what are often called retentions. And I guess I alluded to this earlier, when I spoke about these things that come out of Africa, which are retained by African Americans despite everything that we've gone through here in this part of the world. But, I would also say that Hip Hop coalesces around certain social realities. So, it coalesces in New York City, when you have infrastructure that's falling apart, and it's kind of left to the people of the city to make what they will of it. There's that famous *New York Daily News* cover that says, "FORD TO CITY: DROP DEAD."[2] This was talking about how the Federal government was not going to bail out New York, which was going through immense financial troubles, at that time. I would also say that Hip Hop speaks to a kind of accessibility to and familiarity with technological tools, especially electronic ones. You have to get to a certain place in the story of electronic tools and, and how you get them, and how you use them, before you can do things like put your hand on a turntable or on a record platter. You wouldn't have done that with a gramophone. That was the kind of thing you would put up, lock up. A lot of artists, a lot of DJs, talk about the struggle that they had with their parents to get access to the records. That's often a big part of how DJs talk about their early years—"Dad wouldn't let me touch the records" or "He told me never to touch those records." But at the same time, what you often find is that the parents of DJs were people who often had a lot of social gatherings at their homes. Their father might have been an aspiring DJ, playing records in the neighborhood. So, you're talking about a certain kind of collecting, which is taking place at that time. It's only after a certain kind of, if you will, commercialization and distribution processes are consolidated that someone can become a collector of records. And I would also add that, interestingly enough, Hip Hop is founded by three people—three DJs, Kool Herc, Grandmaster flash, and Afrika Bambaataa. They are first generation, or immigrants, first-generation Americans—their parents come from the West Indies, where there are already certain kinds of practices going on with record playing and music that they were able to further develop. And I would also add that I think Hip Hop sounds like the city. It's not the kind of music that you would have heard develop in the countryside, or by a quiet brook, if you will. It sounds punchy, percussive, and loud. It screeches like the #5 train, going uptown. I think it's imprinted in time, in place, and by people. That's what makes it sound the way it did. And then, of course, that sound developed as people began to practice and interact with it.

Anthony: Let me suggest something and you respond. It seems to me the music of people of African descent always involves movement of individual bodies and movement of the collective. Mindful of that, what I'd like to suggest is that with Hip Hop you get a reaction to the Great Migration—the failures of the Great Migration. Black people after the civil war move into southern and northern cities and toward the west, and this takes place through much of the 20th century. The blues speak about the Great Migration, and through the blues you get folks talking about this movement, being somewhat suspicious of it but allowing for some hope that it will mean something. The generation that gives us Hip Hop has experienced the failures of the Great Migration. And what you get in their music is signification of that movement and its unfulfilled promises.

Harry: Yes, I think this is all very plausible. There's a mentor of mine who says that the things the racists can always do to nonwhite people are, one, move as many of them as they want and, two, kill as many of them as they want. So, I think that from the slave ships, at least, what you have is Black people being moved or moved about, landed, set, if you will, in a certain place, and then responding. And the setting forms a kind of compression and release, you might say, the compression of the new setting and then the release of how we feel about it.

Dr. Strobert told me that in African cultures there were catalogs of music for expressing one's feelings for one's friends—African catalogs of music could be that specific that we have a section and it's just about friends, and what they mean to us. This is like what the rap group Whodini would tell us about the value of friends.³ This tells me that these are cultures that navigate musically all kinds of stuff, that music is a way to make sense of reality and also, if you will, consolidate the group around a vision of what is actually happening. So, what you've described sounds extremely plausible to me because when we think about it, all those migrations are followed by great leaps in terms of musical expression, and organization.

Anthony: To add to that, it seems to me there are ways in which Hip hop has been self-conscious in terms of its commitment to articulating the movement of Black and brown people. Think of the Slab where I am in Houston. Hip Hop responds to these cars moving slowly through the Third Ward or the Fifth Ward. Or, on the West coast, Hip Hop responds to cars moving slowly through Compton, through Long Beach. There are ways in which Hip Hop conditions itself to this movement, and one of its greatest gifts to us is the use of cultural creativity to disrupt.

Harry: Yes, yes, I would absolutely say that. As you were making that point about movement, I was thinking about the fact that in Hip Hop, a long-standing piece of its lingua franca is "keep it moving," which doesn't mean literally move, but it means progress. Like, gotta have progress in whatever I'm doing or building. Movement is so much a part of style. It's so much a part of Black style also, like, how one moves is connected to rhythm, again. These things are interlocked and linked. Absolutely. So, yes, I think that makes a lot of sense. Disruption is what we memorialize and accentuate through Hip Hop production, ultimately via the sampler and turntable and the use of the scratch.

Anthony: When you talk in terms of the turntable, when you talk in terms of graffiti—these are two elements that point out the poetic quality of Hip Hop. And by poetic I mean to say Hip Hop destroys language—destroys traditional ways of communicating—in order to free it to tell a different story. With the turntable you have the destruction of its initial intent, a destruction of the initial use of the album. And with graffiti, you have a signifying of art and the artistic process—what it entails and who gets to participate in that process.

Harry: And how one views it.

Anthony: Yes, and where one views it.

Harry: I don't remember who it was, but someone shared with me the idea of an African museum being one where you put the objects on the path that you walk to get water. And it is interesting to me that the trains are tagged in

New York by graffiti artists; these trains reversed the interaction with art in the sense that the art would come to you, pause in front of you, and then move along before the next piece would then come along—either on the next car or on the next train. So yeah, these are processes of inversion. And certainly, of deconstruction. I wouldn't say Hip Hop destroys language, but it certainly disrupts it and reformulates it, and that reformulation and disruption is part of the brilliance of it and even part of how one can be marked as a brilliant emcee.

Anthony: I'd want to push the destruction element. In using the concept of destruction, I mean to name a positive development, a positive interaction. Language that was used to terrify and misname Black people is disrupted and mangled in such a way that it isn't recognizable in terms of its first use. And in doing this, language is freed to ask different questions, to point out different possibilities: What is art? Who gets to produce it? How do words get used? It seems to me those are productive elements, productive possibilities we wouldn't have without Hip Hop.

Harry: I definitely agree with you in terms of these goals and these cultural products that you've just described. It's just that the word "destruction" means something different to me. There are so many times I think about Hip Hop, and I say, well, at the end, you're still speaking English. Unless you've gotten something that's completely unintelligible from English, and I don't think many artists move toward that. But I think that at the very least, it's African American English, which closely aligns itself with those patterns and ways of expression. So, I'm not sure I would say destroy, to me destroy really means you don't leave anything behind you recognize, or where you recognize just enough to be able to recognize it's been destroyed. But I wouldn't quibble over that. I wouldn't quibble over that definition, actually.

Anthony: Let's stay here for a minute before moving on. I think there are ways in which one can say destruction is the freeing of language from the traditional rules of grammar—that Hip Hop pushes language against traditional use, traditional regulations. And this gets pushed even further if you think in terms of mumble rap, for example.

Harry: Yes, yes, I definitely agree with that. I definitely see the goal of MCs—some more than others—to really reorganize, if you will, the feel of the language. And what that requires in terms of specific techniques varies in terms of the way you approach rhyming, where you're from, your own vocabulary, your subject matter. So, I definitely agree with that. I definitely agree that it's a form of customization that artists are always seeking. You want the verbiage to fit you—you especially. Yes, which is very expressive.

Anthony: Yes, and breaking it down to sound. You get something like Master P's, "uhh! Na, nah na nah. Make 'em say, uhh."

Harry: Yes, it's very expressive.

Anthony: Yes, for people in the culture, it communicates something!

Harry: Yes, and especially if you use it at the right time. That timing is also very important.

Anthony: Based on this conversation, we have to say that this culture is intentional. Something about this culture is intentional. I want to believe part of that intentionality has to do with morality and ethics that Hip Hop is producing. It is discussing a moral and ethical viewpoint. That is to say, Hip Hop is producing a certain set of values.

Harry: Yes, it is certainly at the service of them. I would say I think that those values and that morality dominate, these viewpoints dominant Hip Hop.

Anthony: Let's drill down a bit. What would you say are some of these values?

Harry: There are probably many more than come to my mind. But I think there's at least one primary value, and five secondary ones. The primary value is the primacy of self, the centrality of "I." I was thinking about this, and I noted that even a record by Kendrick Lamar from a few years ago is called "i"—just that pronoun.[4] It's a primary value—I stand, I see. This is my statement and my viewpoint. I think it's one of the reasons why you don't see a lot of remakes in Hip Hop; you don't see a lot of artists remaking other artists' records. Snoop might remake Slick Rick's "La Di Da Di"" because he's a huge fan, you know, but for the most part, the vocalist is the songwriter, unless they're ghostwritten.[5] The vocalist is speaking about their viewpoint, their point of view, and the idea that even if something is ghostwritten for you, "this is my own point of view" is a far more central value. I am here making the statement, and I stand by my word. I think, in Hip Hop, and even in other forms, in European classical music, when you're not necessarily expressing any viewpoint, you're seeing something that's architecturally profound but it doesn't speak for me. It might speak to me, but I'm not talking about myself when using that classical music. Or, even in jazz, if I'm singing a song, I'm usually singing something that someone wrote a long time ago. And it's beautiful. And it's a classic, but I'm not necessarily talking about me. I think because Hip Hop is present, and also because of the decorative quality it has, there's the primacy of the self, the centrality of the "I." Things originate here where I'm standing, and we radiate out, so to speak.

Anthony: Ok, a type of celebration of personhood. What else?

Harry: Yes, and personal authenticity, and authority. Then there is what I call the unlimited fluency of the streets.

Anthony: Break it down!

Harry: Now, I've been thinking about this idea of the streets, and I wrote to Professor Todd Boyd at USC,[6] and I asked him, "What do we mean when we say the streets?" And he wrote back, and he said, "first, good question," which I appreciated. Then he said, "I think of the streets as the intersection of urban adult life, where sex, drugs and crime merge to create a high-risk environment. One where both transgressive excitement and ultimate ruin define the possibilities." I think that's a pretty good, kind of, like, back-of-the-napkin definition of what we call the streets, and I think the streets are authoritative in Hip Hop. This space called the streets, where everything is real, where there's, as Professor Boyd said, "high risk," and your currency has to do with the degree to which you navigate them and survive them. The streets form that place where, in traditional tales, the young man goes to kill the lion, so to speak. The streets are that psychographic space—the backdrop, and really the only part that feels real in the story.

Anthony: As I was listening to you speak about personhood and the streets, it occurred to me that there's another, undergirding, moral or ethical value and that is awareness. Within Hip Hop culture there is a celebration of and a call to awareness about our circumstances.

Harry: Absolutely, that could be another one. I don't know if I would build it into the "streets" or extrapolate it by itself. But there's that term "caught slipping." That's not good. It's not good to not be aware. I was watching an interview on YouTube wherein Desus and Mero were interviewing Denzel Washington. And Denzel made the point that when you grow up in the city (he grew up in Mount Vernon, which is right near the Bronx), you have this thing where you learn to always be looking up ahead of you to see what's about to happen, what's moving, or bubbling up, right? Several yards up in front of you, you put your viewpoint there. So, I think that thing of awareness, absolutely—where are you? What's going on behind me? What's going on either side of me? This awareness is a big facet of urban life. And when urban life is dangerous, or tentative, even more so.

Anthony: I think that's absolutely right. And I would tag onto this point of awareness another consideration, which is a commitment to raw and rugged truth. A commitment to what is. Period.

Harry: Yes, yes, ferocity. Like the idea that, if I'm making this up, I'm making it up. And we know that, but to make it up and to be found out—well, for example, several years ago, the rapper Rick Ross was found to not be a mogul, but a prison security guard. And the fact that this did not end his career, at the time, for a lot of older heads, was proof Hip Hop had become very indulgent and commercial. The idea was that in the past, if you had found that out, that would be the end. No one would buy any of his boss player rhymes ever again. I think this is an ongoing struggle, because a lot of people say things like, if this had happened before, and they found out that this artist didn't write their own rhymes, that would have been the end of them. But the fact that Hip Hop has become so commercially viable puts these ethics in question—as ethics always come into question when you sit down a case full of money in front of someone. It doesn't even matter what the conversation is, when a Halliburton suitcase full of $100 bills is opened in front of somebody, the conversation changes, it changes direction. And so Hip Hop is affected by all of this as well.

Anthony: Think in terms of the Geto Boys' "Mind Playing Tricks on Me.[7]" This is storytelling. It's graphic. It's disturbing, but it's meant to provide insights that have everything to do with how we think about what's important and how we should behave in the world.

Harry: Yes. Yes. Absolutely. It's cautionary. Even the title, "Mind Playing Tricks on Me," raises a question. It sets you up for what's to come; it's like a great opener. You could almost see it as a movie, with the title card, and you hear the organ blast before we see whatever it is we're going to see. It sets you up for a very unnerving set of stories. It's troubling, and it's also beautifully detailed, and simply told so it shows great craft as well—which is always a mark of the best narratives.

Anthony: And sometimes it's more explicit than in other cases. There's something about Hip Hop Culture, and I'm thinking particularly in terms of rap music, which has the quality of an epistle written to a community. Think about Tupac and Scarface on the track "Smile," or Tupac's ten rules to the game.[8] There are here explicit moral and ethical lessons that are often couched in new personalities. I'm thinking here about Tupac's conversation about Black Jesuz, the patron saint of thugs, who provides a very different moral and ethical code.[9]

Harry: Yes, or Biggie's "Ten Crack Commandments," which intersect drug dealing with the Holy Writ to say this is what you're not going to do, and what you're definitely going to do, and this standard is higher than anything else when it comes to selling crack.[10]

Anthony: This is where it comes together for me—your conversation concerning self and personhood. These values come together in this conversation. There's a commitment to awareness that allows us to understand our circumstances, and there's a commitment to personhood—the survival of something of ourselves despite the circumstances in which we find ourselves.

Harry: I think that there is a fundamental kind of declamatory function of Black music, and a joy about it that has to do with the fact of survival. It has to do with the fact that in whatever era we exist, we understand forces are arrayed against us. And this is not a foreign thought to any of us. I'm here to tell means I survived. I got through it, and this has great power, I think, for audiences and for listeners.

Anthony: I would agree with you, and I would add that there is also in Hip Hop culture deep value given to pleasure. And there are several ways in which you can read that, some more constructive than others. I think in terms of Nicki Minaj, or Salt-N-Pepa, who celebrate personhood and pleasure.[11] It's a recasting of Black sexuality over against the ways in which the status-quo of the United States would perceive Black pleasure. It's a freeing of ourselves to enjoy ourselves.

Harry: Yes, pleasure is the fruit of you having achieved success, and of you having achieved your goal—even if your goal is just to make a pie. At the end of it, you cut a slice, you hold up the camera, you take a bite, you say um. You have to know what all that work was for. And so, pleasure is the fruit, if you will, of surviving, of actually getting through it. That is why so many artists, whether it be in their songs or their videos, show their accumulation of property and of wealth. This is a way of demarcating having been able to get over. This isn't getting over in the sense of tricking somebody, but rather by one's own intelligence and brilliance. And pleasure is now the reward for that.

Anthony: And folks are often critical of that, but we can't lose sight of the fact that these artists are mirroring the American Dream. There is something about Hip Hop culture's sense of personhood and understanding of pleasure that is tied to the US notion of success.

Harry: I've always resented the term "gangsta rap." I always called it "quote unquote" gangsta rap because my position was that everything that rappers talk about in so-called gangsta rap one hears talked about in European classical opera—the pursuit of women, the acquisition of them, power over one's enemies, outrage over undeserved misfortune. The same exact themes are present and make gangsta rap very operatic when you think about it. But it's the fact that it's Black young guys who are so upfront and blatant about it. And you know, there's that attitude that if you see Black kids running through the streets laughing the first thought is what did they do wrong? I don't think we can experience joy on its own terms. There's got to be something nefariously afoot. I absolutely think that it's like taking the American Dream at its face value. But the truth is that the American Dream was not intended for us. We were intended to present it and make it possible for others. That's why we were brought here.

Anthony: Why do you think so many folks have a difficult time appreciating this dimension of Hip Hop?

Harry: I met Chuck D. in college, and he introduced me to Hank, Flava Flav, Eric "Vietnam" Sadler, and Mr. Bill and all those guys. We were hanging out. When I talk to people about those days, what I say is, these were the first people I ever met who took Hip Hop completely seriously. At that time, in its history, the conventional wisdom was that Hip Hop was a fad. It was going to go away. This was what smart people said. It was a given, it wasn't even questioned—No, it's just a fad, and it's gonna go away. We didn't believe any of that. It wasn't even something we discussed as to whether it might happen. We just assumed that this was real and permanent. And I think persons like you—maybe this is why for a long time I wanted to meet you and learn more about you—get it. You're a thoughtful person who's done a lot of work on a lot of questions having to do with what Black people think about. Why do we do these things? And when you look at Hip Hop, I get the sense that it's very clear to you that it's rational. I think for a lot of people it's irrational, so they don't trust it. If people don't think there's rationality behind it, they don't trust it. A lot of people see Black people, especially Black young people, as essentially irrational. They don't know why we're doing all that yelling, why we're making all that noise, why we're so angry. I've long said if you sampled a newspaper over a course of a year, and took all the adjectives that are used to describe Black males and all the adjectives that are used to describe Hip Hop and match those lists, they would probably be about the same in terms of what they say—loud, noisy, maybe destructive, criminal, larcenous. So, I think it's for these reasons, I speak for myself, and I think I detect this in you as well. We both, for whatever reason, are blessed with curiosity. We saw certain things and trusted our own sense of what was right and pleasurable.

Anthony: I think you are absolutely right. And I believe this attention to Hip Hop has to, or should, involve appreciation and critique. We have to be mindful of what it gets right and what it gets wrong. So, moving in that direction, when it comes to life in the United States, what do you think Hip Hop gets right and what do you think it gets wrong?

Harry: I think what Hip Hop, for the most part, gets right, is the reality of race, and how it functions. Fifty years ago, Lerone Bennett Jr. wrote a book called *The Challenge of Blackness*.[12] And in it he said the state of freedom is most accurately reflected in the lives of the men on the bottom. Hip Hop is almost permanently, unrelentingly created by the men on the bottom. And for all the reasons we've just named about veracity and the rugged truth, and so on, those men are compelled to say what they see. So, it's always very strange to me when I see people, usually white people (every now and then, a nonwhite person), but almost relentlessly a white person, talk about race as a fiction or mislocate where it functions. And this isn't something those on the bottom do. It's very clear to them what it is and that it's operative. The artists who make Hip Hop culture get it. Now, they may not use the same language or analysis, or they're just saying it another way, but that race is real and active is not unclear to them.

When it comes to what they get wrong, I would say it's how money works. I think that there's a lot of misunderstanding about what money is, and how it works. I remember hearing one rapper saying how it dawned on him that people who are really rich don't display their wealth. They don't have a lot of jewelry on. For him, if you're wealthy, you wear jewelry and that's how you show your wealth—the ostentatiousness of wealth. I would also say I don't think we understand what women are for, at all. There is a weird coaxially between the saintliness of motherhood and the assumed inevitability of whoredom. I think that these things are bound around each other, this relationship to the female—the mother is a saint, but all of the women are whores. And I think this is extremely problematic. And so, I would say maybe even above money is this problem because when you get that wrong, you're gonna get money and everything else wrong.

Anthony: I would agree, and it seems to me this is where Hip Hop culture connects with the larger culture of African Americans, where issues of gender and sexuality are problematic. It's easier for Hip Hop culture and the larger Black culture to get race right than it is to see and understand the ways in which gender and sexuality have been used to produce disregard.

Harry: I agree with you. But I also think that it connects to the larger US culture in that way as well. I don't think that there's any place in the world where this is not an issue. As a Christian, as a person who believes in the authenticity of the Bible, I'm always struck by the fact that one of the curses that Eve suffers as a result of her sin is that her desire shall be unto her husband. And what this means is that her relationship with her husband was always going to be a source of pleasure and conflict, that she would want to have a good relationship with him, but it would always be a source of conflict. And I see that echoing through human relations today. There is a desire, especially on the part of women I think, for coherence and gentleness, but that desire is often demolished.

Anthony: So, here's one of the concerns for me—and I understand this is a bit off topic. If you think in terms of the Black Church and if you think in terms of Hip Hop culture, both of these major cultural forces have operated with the assumption that what matters most is the well-being of Black people. The Black Church has not accepted the silence of the Bible on issues of Blackness and slavery. I've not heard of a Black church saying it was a mistake for us to seek our freedom because the Bible doesn't say anything about Black people being free. And Hip Hop culture has been critical of the sacred text, the American Dream, US Exceptionalism, the Constitution, but has embraced other elements of normative social reality in the United States. Why has it been so difficult for the Black Church and Hip Hop culture to make use of this same expansive way of interpreting to deal with issues of sexuality and gender?

Harry: I have to admit here, I'm not quite sure I'm clear on the contrast or the comparison you're making between the Black Church and Hip Hop culture.

Anthony: I'm saying both of them have gotten race right to some extent because they have read Black life against so-called sacred stories. They have questioned and critiqued the common story concerning Black people as Black people. Both have done that. Both have read US sacred texts against the way in which those texts were meant to condition and control Black people. But they've not used that same way of reading and thinking when it comes to issues of gender and sexuality.

Harry: Well, I would say that in both cases you have fields which are male dominated, and which are beset by this coaxial of the saintliness of motherhood and the inevitability of whoredom. I don't think that they're different in that regard. I think that where men lead—the Black Church, Hip Hop, politics, business—you're going to see women kind of set up as help. And help means all kinds of help. Whether it means you type for me, or you warm my bed. This is something that men are undone by, tempted by, and inevitably lose their positions to.

Anthony: Friend, one more question for you. So, we are two 50-plus guys chopping it up about Hip Hop. I have to ask this question, what is the future of Hip Hop?

Harry: I think there will be all kinds of styles—most of them nonlinear. I was at Syracuse University, and a student asked me whether Hip Hop had changed since the early days. I said, well, in one sense, it hasn't. Because it's still basically spoken, lyrical, rapping over instrumental beats. If you had died in 1973, and come back to life in 2023, you would still recognize it as rap music. So, it hasn't changed enough where it's unrecognizable. Now, of course, there's an awful lot of modifications in production, in rhyme styles, and patterns. But, it's still recognizable. I think at some point this is going to play out. This is going to be your grandparents' music, as opposed to just your parents' music. It'll be predominantly your grandparents' music, and then it might just be apt for aficionados. And then people will stop updating it, and it will decohere. People talk about Hip Hop being born in August of 1973, but, as my earlier statements might indicate, I say I don't hold to that position. I say it cohered at a certain time, and it's going to decohere at another time. Then it'll just be like the universe which itself will ultimately become irrelevant and decohere everything ultimately does.

9

We're Still Here!

Valerie Cassel Oliver

Anthony: You are about to find out why Valerie Cassel Oliver is a rockstar in the art world! Valerie is the Sydney and Francis Lewis Family Curator of Modern and Contemporary Art at the Virginia Museum of Fine Arts. She also serves on the editorial board of *Callaloo: Journal of African Diasporic Arts and Letters*,[1] the advisory board for the Fabric Workshop and Museum in Philadelphia, as well as the Smithsonian's National Archives. Valerie is the recipient of numerous awards and I'm going to name just a few of them—Getty Curatorial Research Fellowship; the High Museum of Art David C. Driscoll Award; the Arthur and Carol Kauffman Goldberg Foundation to Life Fellowship; the James A. Porter Book Award from Howard University, and the Alain Locke International Award from the Detroit Institute of Arts. She's also the recipient of the Center for Curatorial Studies at Bard College's award for Curatorial Excellence. And what the director at Bard College said sums up everything you need to know about this genius. He wrote, "Valerie should be considered one of America's great thought leaders, a curator who constantly surprises and lightens and broadens the scope of art." So, let's get started. Could you give me a sense of what led you to the art world? What was that moment or series of happenings that made it clear to you, you were a curator?

Valerie: Well, what initially led me into the arts was my love of theater. From junior high school and into high school, it was my mainstay. I was in the National Forensic League and inducted in the Thespian Society. I had lead roles in school plays and won awards in local and state competitions. So, theater was my first love and entree into the art world. The visual arts didn't come until much, much later. The word "curator" didn't have a place in my life growing up. I didn't know what a curator was. And I knew very little about museums, except being loaded on a bus and driven to one. Walking through the galleries as a kid with things pointed out here and there left me mystified. It was a complete mystery how things happened in museums. I didn't come to the visual arts until I was out of undergraduate school and working in a small arts organization called the Black Arts Alliance. I was a program coordinator and responsible for programs that served the artist community that included dancers, musicians, poets/writers, and visual artists. When we moved the offices into a house in East Austin, I began running the small gallery creating small exhibitions with local and regional artists. Even then, the term "curator" did not come into my realm until much later.

Anthony: Say a bit more about when and how the visual arts came into play.

Valerie: The Black Arts Alliance was the beginning. I began as their public relations person and later became a program coordinator. My parents would not pay for me to get an undergraduate degree in the arts, so, I gravitated toward studies that allowed me to be adjacent to the thing I loved. I studied communications with a leaning toward journalism and public relations. Ultimately, my degree was in organizational communications, only because I hated writing on deadline! My studies gave me a platform to talk to other people, to learn their stories, and to share their stories. Then I got this job at this small, arts organization and was able to work with all these creatives—actors, artists, dancers, musicians—people who found extraordinary ways to express themselves. The organization presented plays and events for the expressive artists, but then the visual artists were like, well, what do we get? So, they created a small gallery, and I started programming for the gallery. I began visiting artist studios, and witnessing how they worked—and then it hit me; it was a seismic shift in my seeing and embracing the visual arts. I found the language and process in the studio so very compelling. And I loved the experimentation! So that's what really drove me to the visual arts!

In 1988, the Black Arts Alliance organized a statewide exhibition and invited a guest juror to select the work. That juror happened to be the incoming chair of the Department of Art at Howard University, Dr. Floyd Coleman.[2] I was working with Louis Hicks, curator at the Carver Museum on the project, and Dr. Coleman looked at us both and said,

> what are you guys doing here? Why are you just sitting here in Austin, Texas? You need to be putting your brains and your efforts on to a much larger platform. I want you to come to Howard University and go through the graduate program that I am shaping. And then I want you to go out in the world and really do the things that I know you're capable of doing!

That led me into the formal study of art history (though my degree combined art history with anthropology and theology), but it got me really thinking much broader in terms of how one can create impact on the field and society at large.

Anthony: So, thinking about your movement into the art world, your relationship with artists, and your movement through various jobs and positions, what have been some of the challenges? The art world is not without its issues with respect to race and gender. How have these things come into play? And how have you maneuvered so successfully?

Valerie: Well, I've had many lives in the field. I'm a curator now, but I've worked as a grant administrator in public programs and also in education. And I think approaching various challenges, I bring in all these different experiences in navigating the most challenging situations. The totality of all these various professions has given me not only the ability to navigate the art world but also multiprong strategies (and dare I say, wisdom). So as background, although I went to Howard for a graduate degree in art history, I didn't begin working in museums as a curator. I was a working student, and, when I graduated, I continued my job as a program specialist in the Expansion Arts division at the National Endowment for the Arts (NEA). So, as a grant maker, I worked with a lot of administrators who ran arts organizations that were rooted in community. A lot of the people that I met during this period are actually the same people I work with today. It is astounding that for the largess of the art world, it is still in reality a very small world. I worked at the NEA during its most tumultuous period, think Mapplethorpe, the NEA Four, and Jesse Helms![3] When Congress voted to divert NEA funds to the states, I was part of the bathwater that went out with the baby.

I was fortunate to end up in Chicago at the School of the Art Institute of Chicago running the Visiting Artists Program (VAP). The program allowed me to bring a range of artists to the university from the established and well known to the lesser and under recognized! Artists would give a public lecture and visit student studios to provide them with advice and constructive feedback on their work. I met so many incredible artists and also some really brilliant young artists who were students at SAIC. Artists like Sanford Biggers, William Cordova, Jennie C. Jones, Rodney McMillian, Clifford Owens, and Angel Otero all went to the Institute and were in the very early phases of coming into their own.[4] I was fortunate to know these artists then and now. My life has been about building and maintaining relationships. Honestly, this is the heart of anything and everything. Those relationships have enabled me to navigate the challenging issues when they arrive. When I came into the practice of being a curator, there were very few African American curators working in mainstream museums, very few indeed. Houston was a very interesting exception in that when I came to or came back to Houston in 2000—(I was born and raised there), Alvia Wardlaw was a curator at the Museum of Fine Arts in Houston, and the Menil Collection had not long after hired Franklin Sirmans. So, while, nationally, you could count the number of African American curators in mainstream museums on two hands, three could be readily located in one city. That was a rarity. I always found Houston interesting in the sense that it finds a way of bending ahead of the curve in very progressive ways. And while there was certainly a history of curators working in mainstream museums like Howardena Pindell or Kynaston McShine at the Museum of Modern Art (MoMA) in the late 1960s/early 1970s or Regenia Perry and later Lowery Stokes Sims at the Metropolitan Museum in the early 1970s, Black voices in white institutions are far and few in between. When I was a graduate student, the names I knew were Thelma Golden at the Whitney; Richard Powell who was in DC; Valerie Mercer in Detroit. And, of course, there were others who I am not so quick to remember.

And while there are early instances of curators working in mainstream museums—places like MoMA (Museum of Modern Art) and the Metropolitan Museum of Art (MET)—those relationships were fraught. Black, Asian, and Latino curators were often working primarily in community-based museum and visual art spaces such as the Studio Museum in Harlem or the National Museum of Afro American Art. Those museums were founded so that there would be places where the Black community could see itself reflected. Today, mainstream museums are still making attempts to reflect the communities they serve, so the issue of representation and authorship is still really fraught. As La Tanya Autry has said, "museums are Not Neutral."[5] One has only to look at one museum and two exhibitions to see how representation and authorship matter. The Metropolitan Museum serves as a key example when you compare its 1969 "Harlem on my Mind: Cultural Capital of Black America 1900–1968" with a more recent exhibition, "Harlem Renaissance and Transatlantic Modernism." It boils down to what voices are at the table.

Anthony: So, I imagine you are in conversation with a whole lot of folks. You're moving through the world. All of this has to generate questions and ideas that are compelling. How do you determine which idea can support an exhibition?

Valerie: That's an interesting question. The idea comes from within: whether there are artists whose practices need to be brought into a stronger focus, practices that feel overlooked or need to be reexamined, or simply observations/research that demands a deeper dive; the idea emerges. Now about the exhibition and how it comes into being, well, there are the mechanics of the museum. When I feel compelled by an idea, however it comes into being, I first speak with the deputy director (my boss), and if he likes it and supports the effort, then it moves forward to an exhibitions committee comprised of senior administrators. Museums all have pathways for exhibition making, and at the Contemporary Arts Museum Houston the process was similar, but also quite different. Once approved by this second body that assigns a budget and a time slot, I work with colleagues from across the museum—development (raising money), to marketing, to registration (shipping), to art handling (moving the art around), to getting into the details of shaping the physical and conceptual parameters. There are lots of meetings; everyone has a part to play in taking the "idea" and allowing it to manifest on the physical plane. When publishing in the academy, books may go through peer review. The process is somewhat similar in the respect that you are looking to enhance the strengths of a project and identify its weaknesses. There is support and resources for the project that remains at its core a curatorial directive. When I conceive an idea, I try to conceive of it in its totality, but the exchange is helpful in further refining the idea and giving it shape. Curatorial practice is at its heart a creative endeavor, and I love the opportunity to explore and experiment with ideas and concepts. I do also see the practice as a means to exchange and dialogue about the issues of the moment. I've been fortunate in that there has been great support and enthusiasm for my projects. There has been trust and support, and I don't take that for granted.

Anthony: That's helpful, and I want to dig into that a bit. I'm thinking of the process before you present the idea to anyone. Just in terms of your own internal process, how do you determine which ideas ought to be made public in this way, and which ideas are cool and interesting, but you need to keep it to yourself?

Valerie: The internal process! I am sure it germinates from a space of observation. I may notice things when visiting studios, museums, visual art spaces, collector's homes. I may read a book that I find particularly compelling or listen to music that moves me in some way. Somewhere in my mind the questions are formulating and connections are being drawn. It's not always evident to me. Sometimes I wake up and the idea has just been sitting there watching me sleep! I often write things down—fragments of ideas that require more thought or things that tug at me. Those things may germinate over time into more solid ideas or questions or even convictions. The exhibition, "The Dirty South: Contemporary Art, Material Culture and the Sonic Impulse," for instance, was initially conceived while I lived in Houston.[6] I began working on an iteration of the exhibition while at the Contemporary Arts Museum in Houston. At its core was the exchange between the sonic and visual arts, but it was primarily all contemporary artists and their work in relation to contemporary music–southern Hip Hop. I was looking specifically for a generational viewpoint of what it meant to be "Southern" in the twenty-first century. However, when I transitioned to Richmond, Virginia, and began working in an encyclopedic museum, I had to recalibrate. The city with its history, the museum with the wealth of history in its galleries. It would feel far too shallow to only look at the last two decades; why not delve deeper, and why not a century deep?

Previously, at the Contemporary Arts Museum Houston (CAMH), I could refer to an art historical work, but here I could place an art historical work in the same room with contemporary artists. It expanded, and it expanded in a way that was quite organic. It made sense to expand it. And when I presented it to the deputy director and, later, the exhibition's committee, I presented a far more encompassing idea that spoke more to the African American South that superseded the simplicity of geography. I also looked at integrating different generations (something I've always striven to do), different modes of working and, of course, music of various genres across time. It was about stretching that initial idea as long and as wide as I could, even to the point where I was a bit uncomfortable in that stretch. It allowed me to explore and stretch into areas that I knew very little about. My former colleague, Lynn Herbert, would always say, "creating exhibitions are like educating yourself in public." It should be about that stretch. It is the "creative" part of the endeavor that brings a space of humility, so that you really open yourself up to learning. So, that is the idea and how it begins. That is the internal tinkering. Now manifesting the idea into an exhibition takes a lot of people, and the bigger the museum, the larger the number of people you need to work with to manifest. At the heart of it all, however, is the art and the artists.

Anthony: In moving from idea to the exhibition, and opening to the public, what's the time frame?

Valerie: There is a range. When I worked at the CAMH, the time frame could be as little as six months. Two years is respectable in contemporary parlance, but some exhibitions take a lot longer to come into being. I've taken as long as five years in organizing some exhibits, but "The Dirty South" and "Benjamin Patterson; Born in the State of Fluxus" took nearly ten years from the idea to the actual exhibition![7]

Anthony: Ten years? Wow!

Valerie: Maybe less for "The Dirty South." When I moved to Virginia in 2017, I came with an interaction of the idea that developed through research over a period of maybe a year and a half, two years, and then the execution of it happened within maybe a two-year period. From reaching out to artists, to producing the catalog, to opening up to the general public, I would say that it's been a five-year period working in various degrees on this project. Some exhibitions are quite responsive to the moment, and you can put it together in a matter of six months to a year. There are many types of institutions, and various institutions have different time frames, with some moving slower. Encyclopedic museums generally move quite slowly. If you can imagine a cruise ship with its length and breadth, turning versus a small catamaran turning. It's really that kind of one to one in terms of length of time, and the ability to be reflexive in the moment. Some institutions can move really quite quickly. The Contemporary Arts Museum in Houston was very much like that. You could organize an exhibition and execute it within a six-to-twelve-month period. Here, at the museum in Virginia, because of the different departments and necessity to get on calendar, those things take a lot longer.

Anthony: This is really important. Folks like me walk into the exhibition and really don't have any sense of the thought process, any sense of the labor, any sense of what it took to reach that point. And so, I find this really helpful. But, I'm also curious. So, if you think in terms of the exhibitions you've been responsible for, is there a kind of general goal you have in mind? Is there a particular type of takeaway you want those who come to view to leave with?

Valerie: Generally, yes. For exhibitions that focus on a particular artist's work or the arc of their work, I want viewers to think about that artist's trajectory and how they have continued growing in their practice and, more importantly, their impact on the field. Generally, these are artists whose work have gone unrecognized but who have had a significant imprint. For people who are just coming to the museum, who don't know art history, I would hope that they would see the persistence of an artist's creative expression, and how it shifts and changes over time—how artists provide us with a living testament of who we are.

For more thematic exhibitions, like "Cinema Remixed and Reloaded: Black Women Artists and the Moving Image Since 1970," that I co-organized with Dr. Andrea Barnwell Brownlee (then at the Spelman College Museum of Fine Arts), it's about the role of women in the evolution of the moving image in a museum space.[8] Moving images, film, and video came into museum practices in the 1970s. Primarily what gets pressed forward in terms of the history of this medium, or genre, in the museum is that it's primarily white men who are creating works of art in this particular medium, and material. However, what we did was to focus on Black women working with the moving image. So, it was about not only the evolution of the moving image in the white cube, so to speak, but also the fact that there were Black women who were creating experimental video works or experimental film, women who were really planning how the moving image could exist in the gallery on a monitor, projected or integrated into other genres such as paintings. So, the exhibition was getting to the heart of the material and its unsung practitioners.

Anthony: It seems to me that one of the deep values of art, and it gets highlighted in a certain way through the exhibition, is the way in which art helps us to wrestle with some of the fundamental questions of our existence: Who are we? What are we? When are we? Why are we? And it does it in a variety of ways; but it gets at those questions that, on some level, produce the human.

Valerie: Exactly! When I studied at Howard, I was interested in those questions. My graduate degree was an interdisciplinary degree that attempted to address those questions of who we are, what is our history, and why do we create. There weren't programs like, curatorial studies then or, even visual studies, so I studied art history, theology, and anthropology. I was trying to understand and pinpoint how people were responding to the times that they were living in, and trying to tap into a communal ethos. Artists exhibit the pulse of a community, and how the community is doing and how it is grappling with the challenges that it is facing at any one point. I think we were talking earlier about what drew me to art. It was about storytelling, but it was about telling the story of the moment that you're in. How do you capture that moment? In my position as head of Modern and Contemporary Art at the museum, I am the steward of work created from the 1900s to the present. There is so much history that happens during this period; and, of course, when we look at the contemporary, we are still writing that history. One can think of it as a novel—the twentieth-century galleries and twenty-first-century galleries are sort of multiple chapters in the same book or a series of books that allow us to see life unfolding. Focused exhibitions are extensions of those novels, concise short stories that provide viewers with a beginning, the middle, and the end, all in one complete statement.

Anthony: There's embedded in this, then, a kind of social and cultural critique. And the critique, it seems to me, involves on some level forcing the recognition and the visibility of those who have been marginalized and rendered invisible.

Valerie: Absolutely, absolutely. That is my North Star. That's what I strive to do. It is imperative to build repositories of scholarship particularly around African American art. There is still so much that's unknown. In building this repository you are able to enable generations to come to know the vast contributions of Black artists to the field and the deep impact that they have made. And the field is vast, it is wide and far reaching. It's not flat. It is not a monolith; there is texture and complexity. I think of museums as libraries. You have to contribute to that repository in order for people to understand, to appreciate. It has the capacity as any art form to transcend conversations and notions of difference. And because of that, you have this ability to understand shifting perceptions and perspectives that are not ordinarily offered. Art has the capacity to do that. And it's really powerful to be able to present artists and give them a platform to do exactly that.

Anthony: It strikes me that in some ways one could argue art is always political, but not necessarily in the way W. E. B. Du Bois meant—making a certain social point, a certain policy point, right? But rather, to the extent you have made it available to us, art speaks the humanity of populations who have often been questioned, and marginalized. And in showing their creativity, you show something of their depth of humanity, their worth, their value, and their rightful occupation of time and space in ways that hold the larger society accountable.

Valerie: The idea of the artist as someone who is hermetically sealed in a studio, and nothing else matters because they are just focused on the creation of work is a myth. Artists are citizens of this world. They put their clothes on, they walk out into the world, they have encounters, and sometimes, not always, the things that they create are reflective of the engagement. In some cases, the art they create is the summation and totality of who they are.

An encounter and the artist's response to that encounter can completely shape an artist's practice. Nick Cave, for instance, after seeing the beating of Rodney King, came up with this idea of his iconic "Sound Suit."[9] The work was a direct response to seeing a man such as himself, a Black man, being brutally beaten by the LAPD. For Cave, he was conceiving of a means to keep the Black body safe. In other words, what would a magical contemporary armature look like? How could I disguise and protect myself? The artist, Beverly Buchanan, was responding to the disappearance of and the erasure of Black communities and rural townships.[10] This was in the wake of the Great Migration. People would leave and cities or towns would simply die. She was attempting to document these spaces—who lived there and what the town or homes looked like. Then she began creating monuments and memorials to those spaces that no longer exist and to events related to those who lived in those towns. She knew that with their deaths these events would otherwise be lost. Artists are always responding. We may not recognize the exchange. It may not be a complete dialogue that we can enter into and know, but we feel it.

Anthony: Something about our conversation begs the question of values, and how values get expressed artistically. So, I'm wondering if you would talk about the kind of social values that you have worked to highlight in exhibitions, and let's start with "The Dirty South," what are some of the social values of Black folks you've worked to highlight?

Valerie: Values of Black folks? Well, we are still here against all odds. There is the understanding of oneself in spite of a framing that others would like to present, and while we hearken back to DuBois and the veil, we are still battling this on social media and in politics. I could go on.[11]

There is the social value of joy, of belief, or labor, of resistance. There is the value of traditions made new, of generational exchange. And the last few years have taught us the value of us, and that despite our brilliance and beauty, there are forces that still want to eradicate us. There is the value of dignity that despite this we are still moving through the world with such confidence and grace. We have a knack for projecting our existence beyond the moment that we live in, and we have managed to do this for generations. There is persistence and preservation, and joy despite the trauma and tragedy.

Anthony: That's powerful. One of the things I really appreciate about your work is that it makes clear that the effort of African Americans to express themselves, to place themselves in the world, to speak their existence in the world, takes a variety of forms. It's not just the written word. We have been creative in that way. We have made use of what we could get our hands on and reworked it so as to make it tell our story.

Valerie: That's it! No matter what. And there's something quite extraordinary about that. I had a conversation with Fred Moten about the "cast off" and the impulse to create something out of nothing. For me, that impulse was about a recovery and recouping of something lost. And something Fred said was staring me right in the face, and I don't know why I didn't see it. He said, Valerie, it is "a refusal to see the lack of something."[12] Mindblown! Of course! It is a refusal to see that trash is trash—something to be thrown away. It's very nuanced, but it's very different in its perspective from what I initially embraced. I think that feeds into the larger idea of seeing ourselves. Oftentimes people would want to throw us away, so to speak, and it is a refusal to accept the lack, the fact that individuals or things are disposable. No one, and nothing, is disposable is the original idea of recycling (if one can recycle human life). It is a refusal to see the lack which I think, in and of itself, is extraordinary.

Anthony: Yeah, that is good stuff! As I think about "The Dirty South" and particularly its Hip Hop dimension, it seems to me what gets highlighted is the way in which African Americans have signified. This process of signifying *is* a cultural value that we highlight, right? We've taken things, we've twisted them, we've turned them on our heads! Think about the ways in which the DJ makes use of the record—uses the record against the intended use and the turntable against the intended use. So, there are ways in which we have created an alternate space for ourselves through this kind of process of alteration or signifying, exposing, and shifting. As a collective, we've been the Trickster.

Valerie: It is exactly that—a willful misuse. And because of that, it keeps a certain kind of vernacular. We have a language. It may be a language that's not used extensively by large swathes of the Black community, but *we* know what we're talking about even though we may not know the specificity of something. It's like, oh, that's familiar. So, it is about willfully misusing something as a point of misdirection. In other words, I don't want everybody to know what it is that I'm talking about. I want to select a few people to know what it is I'm talking about. And so, that generally takes hold. I love the idea of the DJ—DJ Screw, if I'm talking particularly in terms of Houston, and his idea of slowing down time, bending time as people who are singing bend notes.[13] There is a particular cultural athleticism. There's a way that we can utilize time to slow it down, to speed it up, to really touch upon a certain kind of feeling, to hit a particular type of feeling of knowingness. There is something familiar, deeply familiar that we connect with.

Anthony: I would add to that the slabs. These cars, these elaborate and aesthetically dramatic cars! It seems to me one of the things that marginalized communities have done is push against the assumption of their utility. That is to say, pushed against the assumption that they are only as valuable as what they can produce for the dominant population—that they are reducible to their labor. With these cars, you get a statement that these cars aren't simply about mobility. It's not simply about utility because there is an aesthetic statement here that speaks a certain type of importance. That speaks to a certain type of occupation of time and space that comes with swag.

Valerie: It starts with the sound system because it gets here long before you see it. And it is a refusal made invisible. Yeah, you're going to see me and you may experience me before you see me, but you will see! There is a particular type of performativity with that. It is again a persistence and an insistence on being seen. I'm thinking about the slab in relationship to an assemblage where you're taking bits and pieces and putting them together to transform something ordinary into something quite extraordinary. The paint job, the rims, the grills, the steering wheels, the sound system. Everything within that car gets transformed. And so, a Cadillac is just not a Cadillac anymore. A Chevy Impala is no longer an old Chevy Impala.

Anthony: Typically, you go into an exhibit, and there aren't arrows on the ground telling you that you have to move this way, or look at this piece first, and then look at this piece next. But is there some advice you can provide folks concerning how they should ready themselves to experience an exhibition? Does that make any sense? What are some of the things they should do to kind of maximize their encounter with the works of art?

Valerie: Yeah, just opening yourself up. Sometimes there's a psychology of how people move through space. And being in a museum, we're aware because it's sheer observation. When a person walks in the room, do they tend to walk to the right? Do they tend to walk to the left? You can create or design an installation very much like people put on sidewalks. Now, I have a problem with people who put on sidewalks because half the time they're putting them into places where people don't walk! You can see where people walk. They create a path where they walk. And so, it is almost like the psychology of that, right? You're on a college campus, and you know where people walk. You can see the footpaths they've created. It's very much like a museum. You do have that kind of understanding of human choreography—where people walk, how they walk, where they want to go. Because of the architecture of the space, oftentimes people can bypass things.

With exhibitions, there is also a conceptual dimension to the design. With "The Dirty South," I worked with then VMFA exhibition designer, Daniel Young, in creating the experience for visitors. I wanted visitors to the exhibition to go through a baptism, so we placed Allison Janae Hamilton's work, Wacissa, at the start of the core of the exhibit—the work is a video projection of images her video camera recorded as it was being dragged behind a boat in the Wacissa River.[14] Therein you see the visuals of what is beneath the surface of the water, and you are hearing water because that's how we got here. There is the split image of what exists above and below the waterline, and because of vegetation, it becomes more difficult to distinguish above from below. It was about a magical realism that defines the South. I wanted people to experience the baptism of the South because it is a sacred space. To me, it is a journey that I want people to encounter as they go through. And the water opens them up to receiving, right? That's what it's supposed to do. It opens you up to receive. It's also just the waterways that got us here as Black people.

Anthony: I'd like to end our chat by giving a little attention to something that was said in passing—the idea of the sacred. I'm fairly certain that I agree with you. I would argue, yeah, that there's something sacred about this. And by that,

I mean there's something about the exhibition that pulls us out of ourselves, out of our individual lives, our individual considerations and concerns, and pulls us into something that is bigger and greater. But I'm wondering what you mean when you say sacred.

Valerie: Creativity is sacred. It has the ability to transform the ordinary into the extraordinary. Creativity has the ability to translate, transmute, and dialogue beyond specificity. It is universal.

There are differences that are stoked to create discord and to obfuscate the reality that we're all collectively human and have the same needs and desires. Art allows us to see the humanity in ourselves through empathy. It really just touches upon the understanding that while we have our specific narratives, our journeys are not dissimilar. We are all human endeavoring in our own ways to be free to be our best selves.

Anthony: To that I'm gonna say a secular Amen!

10

On Black AI

Philip Butler

Anthony: I'm talking with Dr. Philip Butler. He's an associate professor at Iliff School of Theology in Denver, Colorado; and he's the founder of the Seekr Project—a distinctly Black Conversational Artificial Intelligence with mental health capacities.[1] He's also building a distinct Black AI interface combining machine learning and psychotherapeutic systems. He's going to unpack all of that. It's important to know that I typically have to school Philip when it comes to Hip Hop but, today, he's going to school me on race and AI.

Philip: Oh man, Dr. Pinn, thank you. I don't know if I can accept the schooling-me-on-Hip-Hop thing. I know we have had our conversations about that, but I'm definitely looking forward to chopping it up today.

Anthony: For the sake of argument, we'll just say I'm right! But, no, I really appreciate you having this conversation with me. AI is a hot topic but, before you unpack your work, please give a sense of how you got into this work? Why AI and race? What led you to this topic?

Philip: That's a great question. It started when I shifted my gears during my doctoral studies at Claremont School of Theology. I initially went there to study broadly neuroscience and spirituality. But my coursework was bookended by the killing of Trayvon Martin and Sandra Bland. So, I had to reimagine my work—who I was going to be speaking to; what I was going to do for the folks who claim me. And this is when I started looking at technology because I felt technology is pervasive and increasingly pervasive. We're not going to get away from it. I started thinking about a kind of futuristic approach to things. So, all that comes together in how I work with AI—at the intersection of neuroscience, technology, spirituality, and Blackness.[2] This led me to thinking from a cognitive science perspective. And, then, when I was writing my dissertation, after the written piece, I did a mobile app as the second half of my psychological study. Getting more into and thinking possible future iterations is when I turned to AI more specifically. I started delving a little deeper, and that led me to where I am today.

Anthony: When I think of AI, lots of things come to mind, lots of movies come to mind like *2001: A Space Odyssey*. But let's dig a little deeper. What exactly is AI?

Philip: In a very simplistic way, AI is predictive mathematics. That may sound frightening to some people, but I think in some ways it helps to take some of the magic out of it. When we talk about predictive mathematics, what we're doing is taking historical information and we are organizing it in such a way that we can attempt to predict what happens in coming weeks or months down the line. And this is where data science and machine learning (or Data Science and Artificial Intelligence more broadly) began to meet. Nevertheless, we're really just applying mathematics to historical data in order to infer something about the future.

Anthony: In terms of AI, what do folks typically get wrong?

Philip: I think there's this leap, right? When I post on Facebook, sometimes people in the comments will scream Skynet from the *Terminator*. Skynet! Skynet![3] And so, thinking about these kinds of dystopian futures where artificial intelligence and machines take over the world is a common misreading of AI. I think one of the more recent examples of this would be Ultron, if you're a Marvel fan. Tony Hawk and *The Avengers*, they create this particular mind.[4] It sees all the bad that humans have done, and then it decides that humans don't deserve to live. They create another version of it—Vision—and they put some guardrails on it. Vision and Ultron are diametrically opposed versions of AI.[5] With Vision, it's a kind of human-loving version that works within the parameters of the information provided. And then you have Ultron, this more destructive and paternalistic embodiment of AI that recognized human life's lack of utility—denialism around human action and the way in which humans have treated one another and the planet. Based on this type of presentation of AI, I think people are afraid of what may come. But I think it's also good to recognize that regardless of which version of AI manifests itself in the future, or even in the present, this is not something that will happen by happenstance. There is a phenomenon called "The Black Box," where in between the mathematics and the outcome the machines are doing something that we aren't completely aware of. This can be off-putting, but at the same time there are some very intentional things that people can do—by making good, clean datasets; by making diverse datasets; by intentionally skewing toward historically marginalized communities; by paying attention to what the weights are within the model—what is emphasized in terms of what is modeled as opposed to focusing on reasserting historical mores and disproportionate ways of extending sociality onto people.

Anthony: I read that as a somewhat-optimistic perspective. But, let me take the gloom and doom perspective on AI for the sake of argument. If what you are saying is correct, this work is being done by people. And people are screwed up, so how do people doing this work bracket their social sensibilities, their biases, in ways that will allow AI to do work beyond those human limitations of vision? You see what I mean?

Philip: Yes, I get it. I think what you're curious about is how we make machines that do not replicate the current social reality. And how do we make machines that do not exacerbate the current social reality. Right? This is the question of our time when it comes to artificial intelligence. So, you have wonderful people doing this research, such as Joy Buolamwini, Timnit Gebru, and Safiya Noble.[6]

Anthony: Can you tell us a little about Joy Buolamwini, Timnit Gebru, and Safiya Noble?

Philip: Joy Buolamwini and Timnit Gebru are the researchers that lead "Gender Shades." So, "Gender Shades" is a paper that demonstrates that larger algorithms from Facebook, Google, and Amazon, for example, do a poor job of seeing dark-skinned faces.[7] More specifically, they do an even poorer job of seeing dark-skinned women's faces. Buolamwini and Gebru showed the disparities within the performance of these models, and they were able to convince these companies to go back and reassess. These companies went from really, really bad to having their best performance being something like 70 percent. So, even though they're still pretty poor compared to how these machines are able to recognize lighter-skinned faces (80–90 percent, if I'm not wrong, but forgive me if I am). Then you have Safiya Noble, who does her work on the internet more broadly in terms of how internet searches are skewed toward sexism and racism.[8] So, when you are conducting an internet search, some of the suggested results provided can reassert harmful suppositions about specific people in certain contexts. This is an example of what some might think of as AI going haywire, but, in reality, it's pretty much doing what it's supposed to do if they're using datasets from, for example, Reddit—which is highly problematic in terms of the types of language that Reddit users use, and the racism and sexism embedded within these framings. So, if the AI model is being trained using that type of dataset, you can't expect it to regurgitate anything other than what it is being trained using.

Think about it this way, if you train a child to view people poorly and provide the child harmful dialogue, language, and concepts, then it's going to regurgitate those same things given the chance. Right? That's why it's important to train artificial intelligence (AI) in particular ways during this stage of its development, so that it begins to look at more diverse approaches to what it means to be a person and what it means to take data from people. Keep in mind that I'm not a humanist, Tony, I'm a post-humanist. And so, I distinguish between humans and people. For me, humans are this kind of child of the Enlightenment, this universal construction; it's a static approach to understanding what it means to be. For me, in contrast, the person is a local and complex thing. I think we need to be taking seriously what it means to take information from people and not necessarily create machines for one specific demographic, hoping everyone kind of fits into that demographic. Instead, we need to be making machines right for these local contexts and the various peoples that present themselves in these different spaces.

Anthony: So, how do we guard against this bias in production of AI? There's what ought to happen, but the question for me is, how do we safeguard development so as to make that the case? How do we move to a position of, well, we ought to do this in a way that eliminates bias and makes it a more expansive and useful enterprise and possibility across communities? How do we move from "ought" to this actually happening?

Philip: You may or may not like my answer. I don't think that we're gonna get rid of bias. And so, I think we ought to be as biased as possible, and the guardrails come up when we're intentionally biased toward the world that we want. When people say, oh, we're working toward making a better world, but we're still engaging in the same old practices, I tend to be skeptical of their intentions and the ways in which they are actually going about it. The work that we do at Iliff and the AI Institute involves intentionally skewing toward the ethics that we want. So, we want a world in which we make sure that folks who have darker skin hues, specifically darker-skinned women, are seen by these computers. We care about how these machines understand people, right? There's a concept called a "data mill," where you have a team of three people looking at a picture. If two of the three people agree on what the picture is, regardless of what that picture *actually* is, that's what the picture is labeled as. So, if everyone who looks a certain way is labeled through these data mills in a way that reemphasizes, or digitally codifies negative presuppositions, then, essentially, once it's embedded in the machines, that information is going to be regurgitated. One of the things we're working on is a self-identification, or self-labeled, approach.

When we are asking people to engage in a consent-based model, to contribute to datasets, we want them to also label themselves so they don't get mislabeled by other people. Ultimately, we hope this will allow machines to not only see people as they see themselves but also force the people on the other end who are reading these machines to view the people as the people intend themselves to be seen. I think there are ways to guard against this mislabeling by specifically skewing toward the ethic that we want. But it's also going to have to involve policy. In the United States, I understand that in certain ways it can be the case that industry leads the conversation concerning policy, but I think artificial intelligence is too much embedded in our everyday life, and it will be even more so, in such a way that it's going to require a much larger conversation about what it means to think ethically, and what it means to create the world we say we want, as opposed to recapitulating to what we have had historically.

Anthony: You've talked some about face recognition, but what are some of the other ways in which bias is represented?

Philip: Yes, through language. I don't know how you communicate on social media, but some folks say things that get them put in Facebook jail or Twitter jail. And what we're finding is that the majority of things that land people in Twitter jail or that result in having their profiles labeled problematic fall within Black vernacular or Black ways of relating. So, Black folks are being disproportionately singled out, suggesting that their language and their ways of relating to one another are harmful or against community standards. Right? But you have examples of alt-right groups, or specifically white supremacist groups, who have been allowed to maintain themselves in the same spaces and engage in dialogue and engage in rhetoric, that Black people would consider dangerous, harmful and threatening. The bots within these larger companies like Facebook or Meta don't necessarily label those problematic, and so there aren't the same social media repercussions. This is why things like Black literature or Chicano literature, and so on—these other conceptual modes of vernacular as they are presented in a written form—can be used to broaden these language models so that when they look at sentiment analysis (which is basically to determine if something's positive and negative), there's a broader range of what is considered acceptable.

Anthony: I want to go back to something you said earlier—the idea of emphasizing bias that helps us to think diversity in a more inclusive and productive manner. That's intriguing, so I'd like to push that a bit. What's the sort of values you'd like to emphasize or celebrate through that process?

Philip: I think this is where we start looking at equity as a real thing. When you have a broadly diverse dataset, then you can say, okay, now everybody's being seen. Alright, great! But, then, what do we do with the ways in which these machines, and these technologies, have been used as carceral agents, right? As a means of surveillance, so on and so forth? So, to do this in an equitable way, we're going to have to overemphasize placement and the recognition of these faces in ways that allow for them to be safe and to maintain their safety. But at the same time, that's also going to require a bit more trust and engagement from the same communities. What do I mean by that? One of my hopes is that we move from prediction—AI baselined as predictive mathematics—toward precision. And precision is not so much about targeting and triangulating as it is recognizing and then providing space around what has been recognized. Here's an example. A gentleman was misidentified about three different times and was said to have committed a crime when he was doing something else in a different part of the state. In order to engage in precision, we'd have to address what it means for this person to be a part of this city, and not only a part of the city's data but also a part of this neighborhood's data. We'd then have to recognize that these datasets are localized to these regions, and if this person moves, they can opt for moving their biometric data to the new location. So, you can't say that this person was in New Hampshire if they're living in Denver, or something like that, or looking at something as simple as their plane tickets and travel stubs. This process is gonna require a bit more trust and a bit more engagement. If we're talking about being precise, it's going to move us toward something that gives people the opportunity to be in conversation with machines, as opposed to being at the whim of machines.

Anthony: I'm not the dude shaking my fist at technology, but I want to ask this question. It seems to me secular and religious folks, on some level, understand community as a value. How they get to community and how they think about the constitution of community may differ. I think for secular folks it's a heightened sensibility concerning community. This, community, is what we have. Are there ways in which AI can or does undercut community, undercut relationships between people?

Philip: Sure, it does. But I also think this is two sides of the same coin. It also goes back to prediction, which is about control. Humans are afraid of uncertainty, and, as a result of this, prediction is a tool that is employed to make sure that they can control the variables—and if they can't control all the variables, we can at least know within the parameters of certain variables what has a greater likelihood of taking place over something else. And so, like for instance, with the Facebook algorithm, or Instagram's algorithm, people don't see all their friends all the time; they only see a certain number of people. Whether you actually talk to all of these people in real life, there are certain people that you're just not going to be in conversation with on Facebook or Instagram. This, again, is the prediction piece. If I have all the data I think I need to know about you, then I can also suggest I know you. There's pseudo familiarity that can arise from this predictive mathematics. And this doesn't allow for the type of curiosity and connection building that can take place when people are genuinely interested in one another. But, on the flip side, how do you then use this data to encourage curiosity? To be in a better relationship with people? One of the projects we're imagining looks at taking people's information—self-labeled data, social identifiers people have— and including it in the augmented reality space. Augmented reality is the combination of tangible reality and projected reality. For example, say you walk into a grocery store and with your augmented reality device you can see who's in the store, can determine their belief systems, and what are good topics to discuss. These are ways that you can actually engage in better connection with people, or better know how to protect yourself against harmful elements of an environment. There are multiple ways for this connection to take place, but there are plenty of ways in which technology and artificial intelligence can create barriers between people.

Anthony: I want to stick with this for a minute. I believe we often assume a type of physicality to community. These are the folks I hang with, but we've also understood for a very long time that community doesn't require physical engagement. It simply can entail shared commitments. These are the folks who share a certain set of commitments, but they don't live anywhere near each other—and never hang out physically. Are there ways in which AI encourages or forces another rethinking of what it means to be in community or relationship, and what we believe we gain from these relationships? Are there ways in which the truth of our self-presentation is altered by AI? So, we become friends or members of community with folks we don't know because self-presentation is flexible, fluid?

Philip: The first thing I think about is gaming communities, where people have avatars that are not themselves, right? So, people get to be "who they want to be"; they get to pick their gender; they get to pick their skin color; they get to pick the kind of species they are; what kind of physical attributes they have, and so on and so forth. In this regard, gaming communities, as an example, become the ways in which the world shrinks; but they also allow for a dynamic approach to how one sees oneself and how one can reassess the utility of their relationships. If you're on a gaming team, everyone plays a role, and everyone has their own spin on unique responsibility within, the clique, so to speak. I think there are definitely ways in which you reimagine. But I'm also very skeptical regarding the likelihood of people just ditching physical reality for a place like the metaverse, which is part of the reason why I talk about augmented space, or mixed reality space. If you can successfully weave both types of realities together, then I think you'll be able to heighten the ways that people experience either-or, and in that way make things more enjoyable.

Anthony: You talked some about your PhD training and your thought process during that training and the anti-Black racism during that time. And I want to use that as a way to get at the Seekr Project.

Philip: In terms of the Seekr Project, when I developed the chatbot, I was training it. And I was like, this kind of sounds a lot like me. I told a buddy of mine about that, and his response was maybe it's a Black AI. We talk about the biases within the technologies that are based upon their creators, so, if a Black AI sounds like a Black person because it's made by a Black person, it probably is a Black AI. And given that the majority of our baseline—the personal assistants like Siri or Alexa—are white and female, there's already a racial and genderized component to artificial intelligence, at least AI entities. This became important to me because part of the transhumanist trajectory is to do away with race anyway—that we can band together under one banner of progress. But again, we're leaving behind cultures, leaving behind the specific wisdoms that come from locales, by privileging one over all the rest. I think it's important for not only Blackness to be brought into this digital AI space but also all the other iterations of the global majority. We cannot leave behind the wisdoms that come from these cultural spaces and the bodies that inhabit them. When we talk about Seekr's mental health space component, we're still attempting to destigmatize and render it normal. One of the goals is a scalable method to reach as much of the various Black communities as possible while simultaneously making this dimension of well-being affordable. We want to make certain Black folks feel seen and heard, and that's why it is a Black AI, so folks feel comfortable and represented—able to explore themselves with impact.

Anthony: You know me well enough to know that theism isn't my thing, and the church isn't my thing. But I like what you're saying in that you're pulling on language that Black secular folks are beginning to recognize the importance of. You get Black secular folks talking about spirituality, but not pointing to some type of mystical union with something out there but as a way of connecting with a deep and profound 'earthy' something. You get secular folks who are deeply concerned with normalizing mental well-being, mental health, taking care of ourselves. I like this in that you take these concerns and tie them to a more positive view of technology. And I think there's a lot to be said concerning that. Has there been any pushback in terms of your project?

Philip: There's been the immediate pushback of folks being skeptical. There are these dystopian views around artificial intelligence. Is it watching me and stealing my information? I cannot trust it. But we're not stealing information. In fact, one of the things we're fighting for is data ownership so that whatever you want to do with it you can—leverage it for your own money, so on and so forth. If you want to keep it all sacred and tied up in a vault somewhere, that's also perfectly fine. There are other folks who say they don't know enough about it, and so their initial pushback is mainly hesitancy around it. To address this, we're delving into the consumer education piece. So, yes, there's been some pushback, but there's consumer education, for example, people have gotten more information and some have changed their mind.

Anthony: In terms of AI moving forward, what worries you most?

Philip: That enough Black folks, and folks from the global majority, are not going to get involved in time to really shift and inform what this thing is going to become. We can do all this work at the AI Institute, and form all these partnerships, but what if it doesn't take root in industry, and companies continue to do what they had been doing, shelving new ideas that would make AI more equitable? At this stage of the game, the potential is still wide open. But, if I were to go for the worst-case scenario, it would be that we don't get enough folks involved who are willing to work to set up folks in the global majority. More than 80 percent of the world is not white. Anti-Blackness is pervasive, so how do we do this work in a way that doesn't perpetuate the very things we're attempting to work against? But what if we get everything we want, and it still ends up being something we didn't plan for? We can't control the outcome, but I'd rather have that future that's uncertain than a future where we speed up the rate at which white supremacy moves through technology.

Anthony: Last question. What are you most excited about when you think of AI moving into the future?

Philip: Depending on where you are, you probably either love it or hate it. But I like the ability for people to stay in community with folks even after they're gone. I know folks who buy keychains where they take voicemails from their loved ones who have gone to the other side, and they play them back. Right? Just to hear their voice one more time. But what if you could stay in touch, with the ability for them to respond to anything, while also displaying some of their key qualities? I'm really excited about just being able to connect with loved ones—the ancestors—in this way.

Notes

Introduction

1 Sherry Turkle, "The Flight from Conversation," *New York Times* (April 12, 2012): https://www.nytimes.com/2012/04/22/opinion/sunday/the-flight-from-conversation.html. Accessed September 14, 2024.

2 See, for example, Brad Braxton and Anthony Pinn, *A Master Class on Being Human: A Black Christian and a Black Secular Humanist on Religion, Race, and Justice* (Boston: Beacon Press, 2023).

3 Paula Marantz Cohen, *Talking Cure: An Essay on the Civilizing Power of Conversation* (Princeton: Princeton University Press, 2023), 5.

4 Some might disagree with my framing of creativity, and such a disagreement would make for a good conversation. Afterall, my goal in this introduction isn't to provide a formal theorizing of creativity. Instead, I aim to offer readers situational, or contextual, information regarding some of the thinking informing this project.

5 Paula Marantz Cohen, *Talking Cure: An Essay on the Civilizing Power of Conversation* (Princeton: Princeton University Press, 2023), 15.

6 Marantz Cohen, *Talking Cure*, 18.

7 Albert Camus, *The Myth of Sisyphus and Other Essays* (New York: Vintage International, 1991).

8 Some might find the language of the human problematic—an anthropocentric turn that devalues other modalities of life. Those with this critique might suggest post-humanism as a better framing. However, I resist the turn to post-humanism, or trans-humanism—although at least one of the interviewees, Philip Butler, moves in this direction. I have some difficulties with that concept—and I'm not persuaded it allows for an adequate engagement with some of the issues (e.g., race, gender, class, and racial injustice) highlighted in these conversations. Hence, I don't impose it on the framework of the book as a whole.

9 In terms of the social sciences, see, for example: Robert J. Sternberg and James C. Kaufman, editors. *The Nature of Human Creativity* (New York: Cambridge University Press, 2018); David H. Cropley, *Homo Problematis Solvendis—Problem-Solving man: A History of Human Creativity* (Singapore: Springer Singapore, 2019); Keith R. Sawyer and Danah Henriksen, *Explaining Creativity: The Science of Human Innovation* (New York: Oxford University Press, 2023).

10. https://www.anisfield-wolf.org/2014/10/zadie-smith-talks-creativity-at-cwru-i-much-prefer-writing-at-this-age-than-when-i-was-24/. Accessed September 14, 2024.

11. Genevieve West's edited collection of Zora Neale Hurston's writings bears this name, and she explains what Zora Neale Hurston meant by it in the introduction to that volume: Genevieve West, editor, Zora Neale Hurston, *Hitting a Straight Like with a Crooked Stick: Stories from the Harlem Renaissance* (New York: Amistad, 2020), xvi.

12. Robin D. G. Kelley, *Freedom Dreams: The Black Radical Imagination* (Boston: Beacon Press, 2002).

13. Kelley, *Freedom Dreams*, 2.

14. I address this humanizing from the vantage point of communities—Black communities—that only recently had their status as human acknowledged, a people for whom the integrity of their being is easily challenged and snuffed out often without consequence. It is only in recent years that Black people—my people—were placed within the category of the human (still, some debate whether long-standing conditions in our social world support the idea that Blacks are human subjects) in relationship to other life, as opposed to being "other" life. I also make this claim as a humanist, and that orientation is present in at least subtle terms through this book; but these conversations don't assume agreement on that philosophy of life.

15. Timothy Stacey, *Saving Liberalism from Itself* (Waco: Baylor University Press, 2022), 98. This book was brought to my attention by one of the reviewers of the initial proposal for my book.

16. Stacey, *Saving Liberalism from Itself*.

17. Stacey, *Saving Liberalism from Itself*.

18. See Anthony Pinn, *The Black Practice of Disbelief* (Boston: Beacon Press, 2024).

19. Albert Camus, *The Rebel: An Essay on Man in Revolt* (New York: Vintage International, 1991), 82, 253.

20. This thinking, of course, runs against a general assumption put in place by thinkers such as W. E. B. Du Bois that art—by extension creativity—is already and always political in nature.

21. For example: *Why, Lord? Suffering and Evil in Black Theology* (1995); *The End of God-Talk* (2012); *Writing God's Obituary* (2014); and *The Oxford Handbook of Humanism* (2021).

22. In making this claim, I have in mind Charles Taylor's argument in *A Secular Age* (Cambridge, MA: The Belknap Press of Harvard University Press, 2007).

23. Information related to these summaries in the introduction is also offered at the start of each chapter as a way to frame the conversation.

24. Candace Gorham, *On Death, Dying and Disbelief* (Durham, NC: Pitchstone Publishing, 2021).

25. Christopher Cameron, *Black Freethinkers: A History of African American Secularism* (Evanston: Northwestern University Press, 2019).

Chapter 1

1. Candace Gorham, *The Ebony Exodus Project: Why Some Black Women are Walking Out on Religion—and Others Should Too* (Durham, NC: Pitchstone Publishing, 2013) and *On Death, Dying and Disbelief* (Durham, NC: Pitchstone Publishing, 2021).

2. For more information on Jehovah's Witnesses, see: https://www.jw.org/en/.

3. For information on Darrel Ray, see: https://www.seculartherapy.org/dr-darrel-ray. His books include: *The God Virus: How Religion Infects Our Lives and Culture* (Ipc Press, 2009).

4. For additional information, see for example, Maarten A. S. Boksem, Theo F. Meijman and Monicque M. Lorist, "Effects of Mental Fatigue on Attention: An ERP Study," https://pubmed.ncbi.nlm.nih.gov/15913965/.

5. For information on Restoration Therapy, see for example: Franz Pfitzer and Terry Hargrave, *Restoration Therapy: Understanding and Guiding Healing in Marriage and Family Therapy* (New York: Routledge, 2011).

6. Henry David Thoreau, *Walden and Civil Disobedience* (New York: Vintage, 2014).

Chapter 2

1. For information on these two organizations, see: https://www.sharebaby.org/ and https://americanhumanist.org/.

2. For information on these organizations see: https://generationcommongood.org/our-team; https://www.greenjusticeworkers.org/; https://nonprofit.fund/; https://ourclimate.us/.

3. https://www.famu.edu/.

4. https://www.thehistorymakers.org/biography/bishop-vashti-mckenzie-23; https://www.warnock.senate.gov/; https://www.thehistorymakers.org/biography/reverend-frederick-douglass-haynes-iii.

5. https://divinity.yale.edu/faculty-and-research/yds-faculty/william-barber; https://www.poorpeoplescampaign.org/.

6. See: https://secularstudents.org/; https://chaplains.harvard.edu/people/greg-epstein; https://chaplaincy.tufts.edu/anthony-cruz-pantojas-humanist-chaplain/.

7. See: https://www.womenshistory.org/education-resources/biographies/audre-lorde; https://www.staceyabrams.com/.

8. See: https://m4bl.org/.

Chapter 3

1. Christopher Cameron, *Abolitionist Movement: Documents Decoded* (Santa Barbara, CA: ABC-CLIO, 2014) and *Black Freethinkers: A History of African American Secularism* (Evanston, IL: Northwestern University Press, 2019).
2. Christopher Cameron, *To Plead Our Own Cause: African Americans in Massachusetts and the Making of the Antislavery Movement* (Kent, OH: Kent State University Press, 2014); Albert Raboteau, *Slave Religion: The Invisible Institution in the Antebellum South* (New York: Oxford University Press, 2004).
3. "Black Folk Don't," https://blackpublicmedia.org/watch/black-folks-dont/.
4. Anthony B. Pinn, *By These Hands: A Documentary History of African American Humanism* (New York: New York University Press, 2001).
5. These figures are discussed in Cameron's book, *Black Freethinkers*.
6. James Forman, *The Making of Black Revolutionaries* (Seattle: University of Washington Press, 1997).
7. See, for example, Gary Dorrien's, *The Making of American Liberal Theology*, Vol. 1–3 (Louisville, KY: John Knox, 2001–2003).
8. Susan Jacoby, *Freethinkers: A History of American Secularism* (New York: Metropolitan/Owl Books, 2004).
9. Nella Larsen, *Quicksand and Passing* (New Brunswick, NJ: Rutgers University Press, 1986).
10. James Weldon Johnson, *God's Trombones: Seven Negro Sermons in Verse* (New York: Penguin Classics, 2008).
11. W. E. B. DuBois, *Prayers for Dark People*, ed. Herbert Aptheker (Amherst: The University of Massachusetts Press, 1980).
12. For example: Langston Hughes, "Goodbye Christ," https://www.poetrynook.com/poem/goodbye-christ; Zora Neale Hurston, *Dust Tracks on a Road* (New York: Amistad, 2006); James Baldwin, *The Fire Next Time* (New York: Vintage, 1992).
13. Richard Wright, *Black Boy [American Hunger: A Record of Childhood and Youth]* (New York: Perennial, 1993).
14. David Blight, *Frederick Douglass: Prophet of Freedom* (New York: Simon & Schuster, 2018).
15. For information on Unitarian Universalism, see: https://www.uua.org/.
16. Nathan G. Alexander, *Race in a Godless World: Atheism, Race, and Civilization, 1850–1914* (New York: New York University Press, 2019).
17. Sikivu Hutchinson, *Mortal Combat: Black Atheists, Gender Politics, and the Value Wars* (Los Angeles: Infidel Books, 2011); and *Godless Americana: Race and Religious Rebels* (Los Angeles: Infidel Books, 2013).
18. "Black Manifesto". The text is available at: https://episcopalarchives.org/church-awakens/files/original/c20bd83547dd3cf92e788041d7fddfa2.pdf. Accessed on May 12, 2025.
19. Sasha Sagan, *For Small Creatures Such as We: Rituals for Finding Meaning in Our Unlikely World* (New York: G. P. Putnam's Sons, 2019).

20 See: https://blacknonbelievers.org/.
21 Voltaire, *Candide* (New York: Penguin Group, 2005).
22 I have in mind Norm Allen's *African-American Humanism: An Anthology* (Amherst, NY: Prometheus Books, 1991)
23 See, for example, Nathan Irvin Huggins, *Harlem Renaissance*, updated (New York: Oxford University Press, 2007).

Chapter 4

1 Phil Zuckerman and John Shook, editors. *The Oxford Handbook of Secularism* (New York: Oxford University Press, 2017); Zuckerman, *Society Without God* (New York: New York University Press, 2008).
2 Phil Zuckerman, *Du Bois on Religion* (Walnut Creek, CA: AltaMira Press, 2000).
3 Jerome H. Skolnick and Elliott Currie, *Crisis in American Institutions* (New York: Pearson, 2010).
4 C. Wright Mills was a sociologist who taught at Columbia University. His books include *The Sociological Imagination* (New York: Oxford University Press, 1959).
5 John Stuart Mill was a philosopher. His writings include *On Liberty* (1859).
6 *American Atheist Magazine*: https://www.atheists.org/magazine/.
7 Joseph Smith was a prophet within the Mormon tradition, who is believed to have received and provided the Book of Mormon, and founded Mormonism. Martin Harris was an early figure in the history of Mormonism, who helped to finance the first printing of the Book of Mormon. For information on the Book of Mormon, the holy scripture for Mormons, see: https://www.churchofjesuschrist.org/study/scriptures/bofm?lang=eng.
8 Led Zeppelin was a rock band that began in the late 1960s. Its most famous songs include "Stairway to Heaven" (1971): https://www.youtube.com/watch?v=QkF3oxziUI4.
9 For example, Karl Marx, *The Communist Manifesto* (1848) and *Das Kapital* (1867), W. E. B. Du Bois, *The Souls of Black Folk* (New York: Dover Publications, Incorporated, 2016); Emile Durkheim, *The Elementary Forms of Religious Life* (New York: The Free Press, 1965).

Chapter 5

1 For information on Rick Lowe and Project Row Houses, see: https://projectrowhouses.org/ and https://www.ricklowe.com/projects.
2 For information on John Coltrane and Jimi Hendrix, see: https://www.johncoltrane.com/ and https://www.johncoltrane.com/.

3   Angelbert Metoyer—https://www.angelbertmetoyer.com/.
4   For information on Michelle Barnes and Jesse Lott, see: https://www.thecollective.org/leadership-v2 and https://www.houstonchronicle.com/entertainment/art_exhibits/article/jesse-lott-houston-artist-dies-18258573.php.
5   See, for example: https://www.metmuseum.org/toah/hd/smpa/hd_smpa.htm.
6   For information on Afro-futurism, see, for example: Mark Dery, "Black to the Future: Interviews with Samuel R. Delany, Greg Take, and Tricia Rose," in *Flame Wars: The Discourse of Cyberculture*, edited by Mark Dery (Durham: Duke University Press, 1994); Kevin Strait and Kinshasha Holman Conwill, editors. *Afrofuturism: A History of Black Futures* (Washington, DC: Smithsonian Books, 2023); Ytasha L. Womack, *Afrofuturism: The World of Black Sci-Fi and Fantasy Culture* (Chicago: Lawrence Hill Books, 2013).

Chapter 6

1   See: https://high.org/driskell-prize/.
2   Chrissie Iles and Philippe Vergne, *Whitney Biennial 2006: Day for Night* (New York: Whitney Museum of American Art, 2006); https://www.stationmuseum.com/; https://www.menil.org/; https://high.org/.
3   See, for example, Jonathan Bernstein and Lori Majewski, *Mad World: An Oral History of New Wave Artists and Songs that Defined the 1980s* (New York: Abrams Image, 2014).
4   See: https://www.wearedelasoul.com/; https://atribecalledquest.com/?srsltid=AfmBOoo7LCHETx2uucSbriVU1E4Oeb9J0_x9Omufpqews8TzM-aMkkzw; https://www.discogs.com/artist/132998-KMD.
5   https://www.tshaonline.org/handbook/entries/biggers-john-thomas; Olive Jensen Theisen, *Walls that Speak; The Murals of John Thomas Biggers* (Denton, TX: University of North Texas, 2010).
6   See: https://www.tsu.edu/news/2023/07/tsus-dr-alvia-wardlaw-is-a-woman-of-distinction; https://epconservancy.org/alvia-wardlaw/.
7   See, for example: "The Secret Art of David Hammons": https://www.nytimes.com/2024/09/30/t-magazine/david-hammons-art.html; https://basquiat.com/; http://www.betyesaar.net/. For information on Jesse Lott, Project Row Houses and Rick Lowe, see chapter 6.
8   See, for example: https://www.blackstarfest.org/seen/read/observed/haile-gerima/; https://www.washingtonpost.com/entertainment/haile-gerima-sankofa-academy-museum/2021/09/23/baae53da-1c81-11ec-a99a-5fea2b2da34b_story.html. Also, Xavier Lee, "Slavery and Ambiguities of Diaspora in Haile Gerima's Sankofa," *Black Camera* 14, no. 2 (Spring 2023): 71–91.
9   For information on Du Bois, see Chapter 4 of this volume.
10 See, for instance, https://www.archives.gov/research/african-americans/black-power/arts; https://www.nypl.org/blog/2016/07/15/black-aesthetics

-bam. Also, James Edward Smethurst, *The Black Arts Movement: Literary Nationalism in the 1960s and 1970s* (Chapel Hill, NC: University of North Carolina Press, 2005).

11 See: https://www.moma.org/artists/7926.
12 See, for instance, https://alicewalkersgarden.com/ and https://www.jbhe.com/features/59_richardwright.html.
13 See: https://beardenfoundation.org/.
14 For instance, https://magazine.artland.com/art-movement-pop-art/. Also, Arthur C. Danto, *After the End of Art: Contemporary Art and the Pale of History* (Princeton: Princeton University Press, 2015).
15 https://art21.org/artist/trenton-doyle-hancock/; https://art21.org/read/trenton-doyle-hancock-it-came-from-studio-floor/.
16 See: https://www.poetryfoundation.org/poets/gil-scott-heron and https://genius.com/Gil-scott-heron-lady-day-and-john-coltrane-lyrics

Chapter 7

1 Jeremiah Camara, *The New Doubting Thomas: The Bible, Black Folks & Blind Belief* (Atlanta: 12th House Publishing Company, 2010); "Holy Hierarchy: The Religious Roots of Racism in America," documentary by Mad Titan Productions, 2018.
2 For information on Creflo Dollar, see, for example: https://www.creflodollarministries.org/.
3 For information on the Slave Sermon Documentaries, see: https://www.youtube.com/@camara714/videos. Accessed May 13, 2025.
4 Books by Dr. Riggins Earl include: *Dark Salvation: Ritual, God, and Greetings in the African American Community* (Harrisburg, PA: Trinity Press International, 2001).
5 Camara, *Holy Lockdown: Does the Church Limit Black Progress* (Atlanta: Twelfth House Publishing, 2004); Aloysius Leon Higginbotham, *Shades of Freedom: Racial Politics and Presumptions of the American Legal Process* (New York: Oxford University Press, 1998). For brief information on Dr. Higginbotham, see: https://www.usccr.gov/files/press/archives/1998/higginbo.htm.
6 Jeremiah Camara, "Contradictions: A Question of Fatih," documentary, Twelfth House Media, 2012.
7 See, for example, Frederick Douglass, *Narrative of the Life of Frederick Douglass, an American Slave*: https://docsouth.unc.edu/neh/douglass/douglass.html; W. E. B. Du Bois, *Dusk of Dawn: An Essay Toward an Autobiography of a Race Concept* (New York: Routledge, 1983); Toni Morrison, *Beloved* (New York: Vintage, 2004).
8 Starring Sidney Poitier, *Lillies of the Field*, produced by Rainbow Productions and distributed by United Artists, 1963, and the *Green Mile*, starring Tom

Hanks, produced by Castle Rock Entertainment and Darkwoods Productions, and distributed by Warner Bros and Universal Pictures, 1999.

Chapter 8

1 For a video on Joe and the Junebug, see: https://www.youtube.com/watch?v=JU8FVpt7IB4. Accessed on May 13, 2025.
2 See: https://www.nydailynews.com/2015/10/29/ford-to-city-drop-dead-in-1975/. Accessed May 13, 2025.
3 See: https://www.youtube.com/watch?v=I36VJ2CXiNs. Accessed May 13, 2025.
4 See: https://www.youtube.com/watch?v=8aShfolR6w8. Accessed on May 13, 2025.
5 For Slick Rick and Doug E. Fresh, "La Di Da Di", see: https://www.youtube.com/watch?v=icBflcYZhpo. And for Snoop Dogg's remake, see: https://www.youtube.com/watch?v=QKjwBEMvowo. Accessed May 13, 2025.
6 For more information on Todd Boyd, see: https://cinema.usc.edu/directories/profile.cfm?id=6459. Accessed May 13, 2025.
7 See: https://www.youtube.com/watch?v=IJtHdkyo0hc. Accessed on May 13, 2025.
8 See: https://www.youtube.com/watch?v=DDS7iqrAfdI. Accessed on May 13, 2025.
9 For an example of the Black Jesuz personae, see: https://www.youtube.com/watch?v=NmNjHV6f8Fw. Accessed May 13, 2025. Also the album "The Don Killuminati: The 7 Day Theory" (Death Row, 1996).
10 See https://www.youtube.com/watch?v=ZYb_8MM1tGQ. Accessed on May 13, 2025.
11 See for example, Nicki Minaj, "Feeling Myself": https://www.youtube.com/watch?v=0Kg9xRooTVk. And, Salt-N-Pepa, "Push It": https://www.youtube.com/watch?v=vCadcBR95oU. Accessed on May 13, 2025.
12 *The Challenge of Blackness* (Chicago: Johnson Publishing Company, Inc., 1972).

Chapter 9

1 For information on Callaloo, see: https://www.callalooliteraryjournal.com/.
2 For additional information on Professor Coleman, see, for example: https://www.aaa.si.edu/collections/floyd-coleman-papers-21723.
3 On Robert Mapplethorpe, the NEA Four (performance artists) and Jesse Helms (conservative senator from North Carolina—died in 2003), see, for

example: https://www.washingtonpost.com/news/morning-mix/wp/2017/03/20/behind-the-loathing-of-the-national-endowment-for-the-arts-a-pair-of-despicable-exhibits-almost-30-years-ago/; https://www.thefire.org/supreme-court/national-endowment-arts-et-al-v-finley-et-al; https://www.nytimes.com/1994/06/05/archives/the-nea-four-life-after-symbolhood.html.

4 For information on Sanford Biggers, William Cordova, Jennie C. Jones, Rodney McMillian, Clifford Owens, Angel Otero, see: https://www.artnet.com/artists/sanford-biggers/; https://www.guggenheim.org/artwork/artist/william-cordova; https://www.jenniecjones.com/; https://www.studiomuseum.org/artists/rodney-mcmillian; https://nyaa.edu/graduate-program/faculty/clifford-owens/; https://angelotero.com/home.html.

5 For information on LaTanya Autry, see: https://latanyasautry.net/.

6 Valerie Cassel Oliver, editor. *The Dirty South: Contemporary Art, Material Culture and the Sonic Impulse* (Durham: Duke University Press, 2021).

7 Valerie Cassel Oliver, editor. *Ben Patterson: In the State of Fluxus* (Houston: Contemporary Arts Museum of Houston, 2012).

8 Andrea Barnwell Brownlee and Valerie Cassel Oliver, *Cinema Remixed and Reloaded: Black Women and the Moving Image Since 1970* (Houston and Atlanta: Contemporary Arts Museum of Houston and Spelman College Museum of Fine Art, 2008).

9 For information on Nick Cave and "Sound Suit," see: https://art21.org/artist/nick-cave/; https://americanart.si.edu/artwork/soundsuit-80565.

10 For information on Beverly Buchanan, see: https://beverlybuchanan.com/.

11 See Du Bois, *Souls of Black Folk* referenced earlier.

12 For more introductory attention to Moten's thought, see: https://www.newyorker.com/culture/persons-of-interest/fred-motens-radical-critique-of-the-present.

13 For information on DJ Screw, see: https://www.texasmonthly.com/arts-entertainment/slow-life-and-fast-death-of-dj-screw/.

14 See: https://static1.squarespace.com/static/528e66a2e4b0a636d24ccd51/t/66a823e0fb46bb7636cfa84f/1722295270166/Allison+Janae+Hamilton_Artwork+Overview_Summer2024.pdf.

Chapter 10

1 See: https://cst.edu/news/interest-in-artificial-intelligence-paves-future-for-cst-alumnus/.

2 Philip Butler, *Black Transhuman Liberation Theology: Spirituality and Technology* (London: Bloomsbury Academic, 2021).

3 The advanced intelligence system from the movie *Terminator* sent to kill the one who would lead the rebellion against AI. See: "The Terminator," Orion Pictures, 1984.

4   Ultron was built by Tony Stark as an AI meant to help generate peace. See, for example: *Avengers: Age of Ultron*, Walt Disney Studios Motion Pictures, 2015. Tony Stark is a Marvel movies character. A rich genius, he developed the Iron Man personae complete with a range of high-tech capacities meant to fight for the preservation of the human race. Iron Man is part of a group committed to this goal—the Avengers.

5   See: *Avengers: Age of Ultron*, Walt Disney Studios Motion Pictures, 2015.

6   See, for example: https://www.rollingstone.com/culture/culture-features/women-warnings-ai-danger-risk-before-chatgpt-1234804367/; https://www.choice360.org/tie-post/upgrading-ai-dialogue-prioritizing-women-of-color-researchers/; https://www.business-humanrights.org/en/latest-news/these-5-women-activists-have-been-raising-the-alarm-about-the-human-rights-risks-of-ai-for-years/.

7   See: http://gendershades.org/overview.html.

8   See: https://safiyaunoble.com/writing/.

Index

Abolitionist Movement Documents Decoded (Cameron)   41
Adkins, Terry   86
African American communities   41, 42
  freethought development in   43
African American history   51
  intellectual political movement in   50–1
African American Intellectual History Society   41
African American Protestantism   42
African Americans   107, 129
  barbarism and savagery of   47
  culture   45, 81
  historians   42
  identity   81
  religion, broader cultural influence of   49
  religiosity of   50
African Americans for Humanism   42
African catalogs of music   108
African Methodist Episcopal Church   18
Afrika Bambaataa   108
Afrofuturism   76, 79, 80
Alexa   140
Alexander, Nathan
  Race in a Godless World   47
Allen, Harry   10, 105
American antislavery society   46
American Dream   98, 114, 115
American Humanist Association   31, 32, 36, 37
anti-Blackness   26, 141
anti-Black racism   47, 48, 79, 140
anti-cultural stance   49
anti-intellectualism   49
atheism   20, 65, 68
augmented reality   139
Autry, La Tanya   122

Baldwin, James   45
Baltimore Green Justice Workers Cooperative   31
Barber, William   34
Barnes, Michelle   77
Basquiat, Jean-Michel   4, 82, 94
B-boying   106
Bearden, Romare   88
belief systems   139
Bennett Jr., Lerone
  The Challenge of Blackness   116
Bible   17
Biggers, John   10, 82, 88
Biggers, Sanford   121
Black abolitionism   41
Black AI   133, 140
Black American   105
  culture   83, 85, 86
  history   92
Black Arts Alliance   120
Black Arts Movement   84
Black Arts tradition   82
"The Black Box"   134–5
Black Christians   33, 103
Black Church   20, 33, 47–9, 96–100, 117
  and cultural power of ministers   44
  rejection of   43
Black community   20, 85, 99, 129, 140
Black Conversational Artificial Intelligence   133
Black cultural expression   107
Black culture   43, 50, 81–2
"Black Devil in Berlin"   78
"Black Folk Don't"   42

"Black Folk Don't Do Atheism"   42
Black freethinkers   43, 45, 51
Black Freethinkers: A History of African American Secularism (Cameron)   9, 41
Black freethought   43–5, 50
Black history   42
Black humanism   97
Black identity, integrity of   86
Black liberation movement   83, 87–8
Black Lives Matter (BLM)   39, 97
"Black Music and Musicians"   107
Black music, declamatory function of   114
Black people   27, 97, 106, 108, 137
   advantage of opportunities during Reconstruction   39
   discrimination against   44
   powerlessness of   99
   well-being of   117
Black political movements   83
Black radical politics   43
Black religion   46, 98
Black secular folks   140–1
Black secularism   8, 9, 44, 50
Black women   15
Bland, Sandra   133
Blight, David   46
BLM, *see* Black Lives Matter (BLM)
Book of Mormon (Smith)   60
Boyd, Todd   112
Brillo Box   91
Broken Faith   104
Brownlee, Andrea Barnwell   125
Buolamwini, Joy   135
Butler, Philip   11, 133
By These Hands   42, 46, 50

Callaloo: Journal of African Diasporic Arts and Letters   119
Camara, Jeremiah   10, 95
   Holy Lockdown   96
   The New Doubting Thomas   95
Cameron, Christopher   41
   Abolitionist Movement Documents Decoded   41
   Black Freethinkers: A History of African American Secularism   9, 41

CAMH, *see* Contemporary Arts Museum Houston (CAMH)
Camus, Albert   3, 4, 7
capitalism   32, 44, 62
Carver Museum   120
Cave, Nick   127
The Challenge of Blackness (Bennett Jr.)   116
Christianity   17–19, 44, 45
Christian nationalism   62
Christian tradition   27
Chuck D   115
Church-State separation   37
"Cinema Remixed and Reloaded: Black Women Artists and the Moving Image Since 1970" exhibition   125
civil rights movement   20
Civil War   47
classical theological theory   62
climate change   64
climate justice   31, 38
Cohen, Paula Marantz   2
Coleman, Floyd   120
Coltrane, John   75, 76
communication   29, 60
communicative openness   3
consent-based model   137
Contemporary Arts Museum Houston (CAMH)   123–5
Contradiction: A Question of Faith (documentaries)   95, 97, 99
Cordova, William   121
Cosman, Barry   65
COVID pandemic   26, 32
creativity   131
   disciplinary perspectives on   5
   distinction between inspiration and   5
Crisis in American Institutions   55
critical thinking   60, 62
Cruz, Anthony   37
cultural moment   87–8
curatorial practice   123
curators   75, 119–22
Cyrus, Jamal   10, 81

data mill   136
dehumanization, of Blacks   102

Diaspora religion 33
direct conversation 2
Directed Attention Fatigue 23, 25
"The Dirty South: Contemporary Art, Material Culture and the Sonic Impulse" exhibition 123, 124, 128, 130
disability justice 38
diverse conversation 2
DJing 106, 107
Dollar, Creflo 96
Douglass, Frederick 46, 98
Driscoll Prize 81
Du Bois, W. E. B. 45, 53, 62, 84, 86, 98, 127, 128
Durkheim, E. 62
Dutchin, Nadya 9, 31

Earl, Riggins 96
Ebony Exodus Project 15, 19
economic justice 38, 44
emceeing 106
empathy 35, 64
empirical claims 63–4
encyclopedic museums 124, 125
Episcopalian summer camp 59
Epstein, Greg 37
equality 31, 37–8
European classical music 111
European enlightenment 50
European modernists 82
Executive Advisory Council 37

Fabric Workshop and Museum, Philadelphia 119
"Face of God" 77, 78
First World War 47
Foreman, James 49
Forman, James 45
    The Making of black Revolutionaries 43
For Small Creatures Such as We (Sagan) 49
Freedom Dreams (Kelley) 5
Freedom from Religion Foundation conference 47
FreeThinkers (Jacoby) 44
freethought

development in African American communities 43
misconception 50

gaming communities 139–40
gangsta rap 115
Gebru, Timnit 135
"Gender Shades" 135
Gerima, Haile 83
Geto Boys 113
God 18–20, 23, 24
    existence of 46
    and religion 17
    slavery with idea of 42
Godless Americana (Hutchinson) 47–8
"God's Arkestra" 77, 78, 80
god virus 19
Gorham, Candace 9, 15
    On Death, Dying and Disbelief 9, 15, 16, 21
graffiti 107, 109, 110
Grandmaster flash 108
Great Migration 108, 127
grief/grieving 21, 24
    while disbelieving 15–29

Hamilton, Alison Janae 130
Hammons, David 82
Harlem Renaissance 51
Harris, Martin 60
Harrison, Hubert 44
Haynes, Freddie 34
Helms, Jesse 121
Hendrix, Jimi 75, 76
Herbert, Lynn 124
Herb Memorial Union 57
Hicks, Louis 120
Higginbotham, Leon
    Shades of Freedom 97
Hip Hop 105, 107
    commercially viable 113
    concept of destruction 109, 110
    conventional wisdom 115
    culture 10–11, 116, 117
    future of 118
    Great Migration 108
    morality and ethics 111
    movement of 109

orality OF   105–6
primary value   111
Holiday, Billie   93
Holy Hierarchy (documentaries)   95–7, 99–101
Holy Lockdown (Camara)   96
Hughes, Langston   45
human creativity   3–8
   place of religion in   7
   processes and patterns of   4
humanism   8, 20, 32, 48, 97
humanist identity   18–19
humanist movement   33–6, 39
humanists   8, 9, 15, 18–23, 40
human values and morality   46
Hurston, Zora Neale   5, 45
Hutchinson, Sikivu   63
   Godless Americana   47–8
   Mortal Combat: Black Atheists, Gender Politics, and the Value Wars   47–8

"Icon Execution"   75
imagination, materialization of   3
imaginative processes   3, 6
imperialism   44
"Inner Necessity to Outer Time"   91
Institute for the Study of Secularism, Society, and Culture   65
insular approach   7
integrity, Black identity of   86
Interdenominational Theological Center, Atlanta   96
involuntary association   6

Jacoby, Susan
   FreeThinkers   44
Jehovah's Witnesses   15–17
Jewish student union   59
Jim Crow   19, 42, 102
Johnson, James Weldon   45
Jones, Jennie C.   121

Kelley, Robin
   Freedom Dreams   5
King, Jr., Martin L.   92, 102
King, Rodney   127
Kool Herc   108

Lamar, Kendrick   111
Larson, Nella
   Quicksand   44
Lawrence, Jacob   82
Lord, Audrey   37
Lott, Jesse   77, 82
Lowe, Rick   71, 77, 82

"making" involve   3, 5
The Making of black Revolutionaries (Forman)   43
"Map for entering and exiting the body"   77–8
Martin, Trayvon   133
Marx, K.   62
Master of Fine Arts programs   85
Mays, Benjamin   42
McKenzie, Vashti   34
McMillian, Rodney   121
Meadows, Mark   62
Menil Collection   122
Methodism   18
Metoyer, Angelbert   10, 71, 72
Metropolitan Museum of Art (MET)   122
Mill, John Stuart   56
Mills, C. Wright   55
morality
   and ethics that Hip Hop   111
   human values and   46
Mormonism   59–60
Morrison, Toni   98
Mortal Combat: Black Atheists, Gender Politics, and the Value Wars (Hutchinson)   47–8
Moten, Fred   128
mourning   23, 26, 29
Museum of Fine Arts, in Houston   122
Museum of Modern Art (MoMA)   122

National Endowment for the Arts (NEA)   121
nationalism   62
National Museum of Afro American Art   122
nature, spending time in   25
The New Doubting Thomas (Camara)   95

New Wave music 81
Noble, Sophia 135
Nonprofit Industrial Complex 31
nontheistic ritual 23

Oliver, Valerie Cassel 11, 119
On Death, Dying and Disbelief (Gorham) 9, 15, 16, 21
Only Sky Media 8
Otero, Angel 121
Our Climate Education Fund 31
Owens, Clifford 121
The Oxford Companion to Secularism (Zuckerman) 53

Patterson, Louise Thompson 44
pattin' juba 106
pay property taxes 48
"Pinn Drop" 8
Pinn, Tony 19
podcasts 8–11
political activism 43
political engagement 43
Poor People's Campaign 34
Powell, Richard 122
precision 138
"Pride Frieze-Jerry White's Record Shop" 90
pseudo familiarity 139
Puritanism 41

Quicksand (Larson) 44

Raboteau, Albert
    Slave Religion 41–2
Race in a Godless World (Alexander) 47
racial justice 38
racism 39, 99, 102
    anti-Black 47, 48, 79, 140
    and sexism 11, 135, 136
    white supremacy and 44
raw conversation 2
Ray, Darrel 19
Reddit 135–6
relic/totem 90
religion 19
    distinction between theism and 63

example of 60
God and 17
religious belief 21
religious faith 46
Restoration Therapy 25
retentions 107
rhythm, centrality of 105
Rick Ross 113
rituals 22, 23
    nontheistic 23
    theistic 23

Sarr, Betty 82
Sagan, Sasha
    For Small Creatures Such as We 49
Scott Heron, Gil 93
secular humanism 57, 58
    framework of 57
secularism 8, 43, 47, 64
    critiques of 50
Secularism and Nonreligion journal 65
"Secularism and Skepticism" class 60
Secularity Research Network, in England 65
Secular Student Alliance 37
secular studies program 68, 69
Seekr Project 140
sense of belonging 74
sense of community 23
sense of compassion 33
sense of mutuality 3
sense of religious suffering 104
sense of standardization 22
sense of vision 5
sense of vulnerability 19
Senufo sculpture 78
Sesame Street 105
Shades of Freedom (Higginbotham) 97
ShareBaby 31
Siri 140
Sirmans, Franklin 122
skepticism 60, 64, 65
Slave Religion (Raboteau) 41–2
slavery 39
    with idea of God 42

slave sermon documentaries 96
slave trade 47
Slick Rick 111
Smith, Joseph 60
   Book of Mormon 60
Smith, Zadie 5
Smithsonian's National Archives 119
social justice 31, 37
social justice organization 35
Society Without God (Zuckerman) 53
sociology 55, 56
"Sociology of Religion" class 60
"Sound Suit" 127
spirituality 3, 9
Stacey, Timothy 6, 7
Strobert, Andre 107, 108
Studio Museum in Harlem 122

technology, use of 1, 2
theistic ritual 23
Thomas, Ginny 62
Thomas, Mandisa 50
Thoreau, H. D
   Walden 26–7
To Plead Our Own Cause 41
traditional West African
   sculptures 92
transcendentalism 46
trauma bond 19–20
Tucker, Angela 42
Turkle, Sherry 1

Ultron 134
United Methodism 18
United Methodist Church 17

United States
   artificial intelligence in 137
   Black life entails in 26
   humanism and atheism in 20
   indigenous form of secularism
     in 50
   normative social reality in 117
urban sociology 55

value judgment 74
values
   of the church 20
   moral and ethical 73
   secular system of 19
Vision 134
Visiting Artists Program (VAP) 121
voluntary association 6

Walden (Thoreau) 26–7
Walker, Alice 85, 86
Wardlaw, Alvia 122
Warhol, Andy
   Brillo Box 91
Warnock, Raphael 34, 62–3
Washington, Denzel 112
white-on-white crime 38
Wright, Richard 45, 86
writing 106

Young, Daniel 130

Zuckerman, Phil 10, 53
   The Oxford Companion to
     Secularism 53
   Society Without God 53